THE
ESSENCE
OF
RELIGION

Titles on the Philosophy of Religion in Prometheus's Great Books in Philosophy Series

See the back of this volume for a complete list of titles in Prometheus's Great Books in Philosophy Series.

THE ESSENCE OF RELIGION

TRANSLATED BY
ALEXANDER LOOS

LUDWIG
FEUERBACH

GREAT BOOKS IN PHILOSOPHY

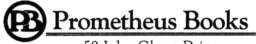 Prometheus Books

59 John Glenn Drive
Amherst, New York 14228-2197

Published 2004 by Prometheus Books

Inquiries should be addressed to
Prometheus Books
59 John Glenn Drive
Amherst, New York 14228–2197

VOICE: 716–691–0133, EXT. 207; FAX: 716–564–2711.

08 07 06 05 04   5 4 3 2 1

Library of Congress Cataloging-in-Publication Data

Feuerbach, Ludwig, 1804–1872.
  [Wesen der Religion. English]
  The essence of religion / Ludwig Feuerbach ; translated and
condensed by Alexander Loos.
       p. cm. — (Great books in philosophy)
  Originally published: New York : Asa K. Butts, 1873.
  ISBN 1–59102–213–4 (alk. paper)
  1. Religion. I. Title. II. Series.

B2971.W5E5 2004
200—dc22

                                                                2004044660
                                                                        CIP

Printed in the United States of America on acid-free paper.

Publisher's Note

During the mid–nineteenth century, Ludwig Feuerbach composed a series of thirty essays, together titled *The Essence of Religion*. Contained herein are the three main essays that set the stage for this larger work. All were translated with notes by Alexander Loos in 1873.

LUDWIG FEUERBACH was born on July 28, 1804, in Landshut, Bavaria, a state in southern Germany. He began his academic career intending to study theology at the University of Heidelberg and later at the University of Berlin. However, he soon became captivated by the dominating influence of G. W. F. Hegel (1770–1831) and studied philosophy in earnest, completing his education in natural science at Erlangen. He received his doctorate in philosophy in 1828.

Two years later, he published anonymously his first book, *Thoughts on Death and Immortality*, which attacked personal immortality and advocated the immortality of reabsorption in nature. Although this view, in part, kept him from academic advancement, his work set the stage for his more influential writings. *The Essence of Christianity* (1841) called religion a form of self-deception. Feuerbach argued that man unconsciously projects his best qualities onto an imaginary external being he calls God. However, practical men, Feuerbach continues, use science and technology rather than fantasy to satisfy their needs. Feuerbach's most important work, *Lectures on the Essence of Religion*, comprises a series of lectures he gave throughout his academic career. In this 1851 work, Feuerbach expands the themes found in *The Essence of Christianity*, advocating the overthrow of religion by science.

With his interests in religion and philosophy, Feuerbach was uniquely able to discuss, analyze, and critique both theological questions and the prevailing Hegelianism of his time. Having set his focus on man's relationship to his fellow human beings and to the world, Feuerbach criticized the idealism of Hegel in addition to recasting religion in general and Christianity in particular from a humanistic perspective. His anthropological interest in human transcendence toward the absolute and the divine compelled Feuerbach to bring these heady subjects down to a human level at which they had a greater chance of influencing the lives of real people. Reason, cooperation, and mutual understanding would demonstrate that the relationship between self and others,

"I-and-thou," is fundamental and more compelling than the faith-bound desire for supernatural communion.

His groundbreaking work influenced such important social philosophers and theologians as Karl Marx, Martin Buber, and Karl Barth. In rejecting religion and embracing materialism, Feuerbach emphasized the biological nature of man, and his critique of Hegel's idealism built the foundation for the revolutionary work of Marx and Friedrich Engels.

Feuerbach retired to Nuremberg in 1860, where he died on September 13, 1872. His other works include *Toward the Critique of the Hegelian Philosophy* (1839), *Principles and Philosophy of the Future* (1843), and *The Essence of Faith According to Luther* (1844).

THE

ESSENCE OF RELIGION,

GOD THE IMAGE OF MAN.

MAN'S DEPENDENCE UPON NATURE THE LAST AND ONLY SOURCE OF RELIGION.

———◆———

[The following treatise forms the basis and substance of the author's larger work, published under the same title, as a complement to his previous: "Essence of Christianity" (translated into English by Marion Evans, the translator of Strauss' "Life of Jesus." It will recommend itself to the unbiased reader as by far the most striking and powerful argument for the human origin of religion in general, and Christianity in particular, before which all claims and pretensions of dogmatism sink into naught.—Translator.]

§ 1. That being which is different from and independent of man, or, which is the same thing, of God, as represented in the "Essence of Christianity,"—the being without human nature, without human qualities and without human individuality is in reality nothing but *Nature*.([2])

§ 2. The feeling of dependence in man is the source of religion; but the object of this dependence, viz., that upon which man is and feels himself dependent, is originally nothing but Nature. Nature is the first original object of religion, as is sufficiently proved by the history of all religions and nations.

§ 3. The assertion that religion is innate with and natural to man, is false, if religion is identified with Theism ; but it is perfectly true, if religion is considered to be nothing but that feeling of dependence by which man is more or less conscious that he does not and cannot exist without another being, different from himself, and that his existence does not originate in himself. Religion, thus understood, is as essential to man as light to the eye, as air to the lungs, as food to the stomach. Religion is the manifestation of man's conception of himself. But above all man is a being who does not exist without light, without air, without water, without earth, without food,—he is, in short, a being dependent on Nature. This dependence in the animal, and in man as far as he moves within the sphere of the brute, is only an unconscious and unreflected one ; but by its elevation into consciousness and imagination, by its consideration and profession, it becomes religion. Thus all life depends on the change of seasons; but man alone celebrates this change by dramatic representations and festival acts. But such festivals, which imply and represent nothing but the change of the seasons, or of the phases of the moon, are the oldest, the first, and the real confessions of human religion.

§ 4. Man, as well as any individual nation or tribe considered in its particularity, does not depend on nature or earth in general, but on a particular locality—not on water generally, but on some particular water, stream or fountain. Thus the Egyptian is no Egyptian out of

Egypt; the Indian is no Indian out of India. For this very reason those ancient nations which were so firmly attached to their native soil, and not yet attained to the conception of their true nature as members of mankind, but which clung to their individuality and particularity as nations and tribes, were fully justified in worshiping the mountains, trees, animals, rivers and fountains of their respective countries as divine beings; for their whole individuality and existence were exclusively based upon the particularity of their country and its nature—just as he who recognizes the universe as his home, and himself as a part of it, transfers the universal character of his being into his conception of God.

§ 5. It is a fantastic notion that man should have been enabled only by "Providence," through the assistance of "superhuman" beings, such as Gods, Spirits, Genii and Angels, to elevate himself above the state of the animal. Of course man has become what he is not through himself alone; he needed for this the assistance of other beings. But these were no supernatural creatures of imagination, but real, natural beings—no beings standing above but below himself, for in general every thing that aids man in his conscious and voluntary actions, commonly and pre-eminently called human, every good gift and talent, does not come from above, but from below; not from on high, but from the very depths of Nature. Such assistant beings, such tutelary genii of man, are especially the animals. Only through them man raised himself above them; only by their protection and assistance, the seed of human perfection could grow. Thus we read in the book of Zendavesta, and even in its very oldest and most genuine part, Vendidad: "Through the intellect of the dog is the world upheld.

If he did not protect the world, thieves and wolves would rob all property." This importance of the animals to man, particularly in times of incipient civilization, fully justifies the religious adoration with which they are looked upon. The animals were necessary and indispensable to man ; on them his human existence depended —but on what his life and existence depends, that is his God. If the Christian no longer adores Nature as God, it is only because in his belief his existence does not depend on Nature, but on the will of a being different from Nature ; but still he considers and adores this being as a divine, *i. e.* supreme being, only because he deems it to be the author and preserver of his existence and life. Thus the worship of God depends only on the self-adoration of man, and is nothing but the manifestation of the latter ; for suppose I should despise myself and my life—and man originally and normally does not make any distinction between himself and his life—how should I praise and worship that upon which such pitiful and contemptible life depends? The value which I consciously attribute to the source of life reflects therefore only the value which I unconsciously attribute to life and myself. The higher therefore the value of life, the higher also the value and dignity of those who give life, viz. of the Gods. How could the Gods possibly be resplendent in gold and silver, unless man knew the value and the use of gold and silver? What a difference between the fullness and love of life among the Greeks, and the desolation and contempt of life among the Indians—but at the same time what a difference between the Greek and Indian mythology, between the Olympian father of the Gods and of man and the huge Indian opossum or the rattlesnake—the ancestor of the Indians!

§ 6. The Christian enjoys life just as much as the Heathen, but he sends his thankofferings for the enjoyments of life upward to the father in Heaven: he accuses the Heathen of idolatry for the very reason that they confine their adoration to the creature and do not rise to the first cause as the only true cause of all benefits. But do I owe my existence to Adam, the first man? Do I revere him as my parent? Why shall I not stop at the creature? Am I myself not a creature? Is not the very nearest cause which is equally defined and individual with myself, the last cause for me, who myself am not from afar, as I myself am a defined and individual being? Does not my individuality, inseparable and undistinguishable as it is from myself and my existence, depend on the individuality of my parents? Do I not, if I go further back, at last lose all traces of my existence? Is there not a necessary limit to my thus going back in search of the first cause? Is not the beginning of my existence absolutely individual? Am I begotten and conceived in the same year, in the same hour, with the same disposition, in short under the same internal and external conditions as my brother? Is not therefore my origin just as individually my own as my life without contradiction is my own life? Shall I therefore extend my filial love and veneration back to Adam? No, I am fully entitled to stop with my religious reverence at those things which are nearest to me, viz., my parents, as the cause of my existence.

§ 7. The uninterrupted series of the finite causes or objects, so-called, which was defined by the Atheists of old as an infinite and by the Theists as a finite one, exists only in the thoughts and the imagination of man, like time, in which one moment follows another without interruption or distinction. In reality the tedious monotony of this causal series is interrupted and destroyed by the difference and individuality of the objects, which individuality causes each by itself to appear new, independent, single, final and absolute. Certainly water, which in the conception of natural religion is a divine being, is on the one hand a compound, depending on hydrogen and oxygen, but at the same time it is something new, to be compared to itself only, and original, wherein the qualities of its two constituent elements, as such, have disappeared and are destroyed. Certainly the moonlight, which the Heathen, in his religious simplicity, adored as an independent light, is derived from the immediate light of the sun, but at the same time, different from the latter, the peculiar light of the moon, changed and modified by the moon's resistance, and therefore a light which could not exist without the moon, and whose particularity has its source only in her. Certainly the dog, whom the Persian addresses in his prayers as a beneficial and therefore divine being on account of his watchfulness, his readiness to oblige and his faithfulness, is a creature of Nature, which is not what he is through himself; but still it is only the dog himself, this particular and no other being, which possesses those qualities that call for my veneration. Shall I now in recognition of these qualities look up to the first and general cause, and turn my back on the dog? But the general cause is without distinction just as much the cause of the friendly dog as of the hostile wolf, whose existence I am obliged to destroy, in spite of the general cause, if I will sustain the better right of my own existence.

§ 8. The Divine Being which is revealed in Nature,

is nothing but Nature herself, revealing and representing herself with irresistible power as a Divine Being. The ancient Mexicans adored among their many Gods also a God (or rather a Goddess) of the salt. This God of the salt may reveal to us in a striking exemplification the God of Nature in general. The salt (rock-salt) represents in its economical, medicinal and other effects, the usefulness and beneficence of Nature, so highly praised by the Theists ; in its effect on the eye, in its colors, its brilliancy and transparency, her beauty ; in its crystalline structure and form, her harmony and regularity ; in its composition of antagonistic elements, the combination of the opposite elements of Nature into one whole — a combination which by the Theists was always considered as an unobjectionable proof for the existence of a ruler of Nature, different from her, because in their ignorance of Nature they did not know that antagonistic elements and things are most apt to attract one another and combine into a new whole. But what now is the God of the salt ? That God whose domain, existence, manifestation, effects and qualities are contained in the salt ? Nothing but the salt itself which appears to man on account of its qualities and effects as a divine, i. e., as a beneficent, magnificent, praiseworthy and admirable being. Homer expressively calls the salt divine. Thus, as the God of the salt is only the impression and expression of the deity or divinity of the salt, so also is the God of the world or of Nature in general, only the impression and expression of Nature's divinity.

§ 9. The belief that in Nature another being is manifested, distinct from Nature herself, or that Nature is filled and governed by a being different from herself, is in reality identical with the belief that spirits, demons, devils &c. manifested themselves through man, at least in a certain state, and that they possess him; it is in very truth the belief, that Nature is possessed by a strange, spiritual being. And indeed Nature, viewed in the light of such a belief, is really possessed by a spirit, but this spirit is the spirit of man, his imagination, his soul, which transfers itself involuntarily into Nature and makes her a symbol and mirror of his being.

§ 10. Nature is not only the first and original object but also *the lasting source, the continuous, although hidden background of religion.* The belief that God, even when he is imagined as a supernatural being, different from Nature, is an object existing outside of man, an objective being, as the philosophers call it; this belief has its only source in the fact, that the objective being, which really exists outside of man, viz., the world or Nature, is originally God. The existence of nature is not, as Theism imagines, based upon the existence of God but *vice versa*, the existence of God, or rather the belief in his existence, is only based upon the existence of Nature. You are obliged to imagine God as an existing being, only because you are obliged by Nature herself to pre-suppose the existence of Nature as the cause and condition of your existence and consciousness, and the very first idea connected with the thought of God is nothing but the very idea that he is the existence preceding your own and presupposed to it. Or, the belief that God exists absolutely outside of man's soul and reason, no matter whether man exists or not, whether he contemplates him or not, whether he desires him or not—this belief or rather its object, does not reflect anything to your imagination but Nature, whose existence is not based upon the existence of man, much less upon the action of the human intellect and imagination. If, therefore, the theologians, particularly the Rationalists, find the honor of God pre-eminently in his having an existence independent of man's thoughts, they may consider that the honor of such an existence likewise must be attributed to the Gods of blinded Heathenism, to the stars, stones and animals, and that in this respect the existence of their God does not differ from the existence of the Egyptian Apis.

Those qualities which imply and express the *difference* between the divine being and the human being or at least the human individual, are originally and implicitly only qualities of *Nature.* God is the most powerful or rather the *almighty* being, i. e., he can do what man is not able to do, what infinitely surpasses his powers, and what therefore inspires him with the humiliating feeling of his limitedness, weakness and nullity. "Canst thou," says God to Job, "bind the sweet influences of Pleiades or loose the bands of Orion? Canst thou send lightnings, that they may go unto thee and say, here we are? Hast thou given the horse strength? Does the hawk fly by thy wisdom; Hast thou an arm like God, or canst thou thunder with a voice like Him?" No, *that* man cannot do, with the thunder the human voice cannot be compared. But what power is manifest in the power of the thunder, in the horse's strength, in the flight of the hawk, in the restless course of the Pleiades? *The power of Nature.*

God is an *eternal* being. But in the Bible itself we read: "One generation passeth away and another generation cometh: but the earth abideth forever." In the books of Zendavesta, sun and moon are expressively called "*immortal*," on account of their duration. And a Peruvian Inca said to a Dominican monk, " You adore a God who died on the cross, but I worship the Sun which never dies."

God is the *all-kind* being, "*for* he maketh the sun to rise on the evil and on the good, and sendeth rain on the just and on the unjust;" but that being which does not distinguish between good and evil, between just and unjust, which distributes the enjoyments of life not according to moral merits ; which in general impresses man as a kind being, because its effects, such as for instance the refreshing sunlight and rain-water are the sources of the most beneficial sensations : that being is Nature.

God is an *all-embracing, universal and unchangeable* being ; but it is also *one and the same* sun which shines for all men and beings on the earth ; it is *one and the same* sky which embraces them all ; *one and the same* earth which bears them all. " That there is one God," says Ambrosius, " is proved by common Nature : for there is only *one* world," " just as the sun, the sky, the moon, the earth and the sea are common to all," says Plutarch, " although they are differently called by each one, so exists also one spirit, who rules the universe, but he has different names and is worshipped in different ways."

God " dwelleth not in temples made with hands," but Nature neither. Who can enclose the light, the sky, the sea, within human limits? The ancient Persians and Germans worshipped only Nature, but they had no temples. The worshipper of Nature finds the artificial, well-measured halls of a temple or of a church too narrow, too sultry ; he feels at his ease only under the lofty, boundless sky which appears to the contemplation of his senses.

God is that being which cannot be defined with human measure, a *great, immeasurable, infinite* being; but he is such a being only because his work, the universe, is great, immeasurable and infinite, or at least appears to be so. The work praises its master: the magnificence of the creator has its origin only in the magnificence of his product. " How great is the sun, but how much greater is he who made it ?"

God is a *superterrestrial, superhuman, supreme* being, but even this supreme being is in its origin and basis nothing but the highest being in space, optically considered: the sky with its brilliant phenomena. All religions of some imagination transfer their Gods into the region of the clouds, into the ether of the sun, moon and stars: *all Gods are lost at last in the blue vapor of heaven.* Even the spiritual God of Christianity has his seat, his basis above in heaven.

God is a *mysterious, inconceivable* being, but only because Nature is to man, especially to religious man, a *mysterious inconceivable* being. " Dost thou know," says God to Job, " the balancings of the clouds ? Hast thou entered into the springs of the sea ? Hast thou perceived the breadth of the earth ? Hast thou seen the treasures of the hail ?"

Finally, God is that being which is independent of the human will, unmoved by human wants and passions, always equal to himself, ruling according to unchangeable laws, establishing his institutions unchangeable for all time. But this being again is nothing but Nature, which remains the same in all changes, never exhibiting the vacillations of an arbitrary, willful ruler, but subject in all her manifestations to unalterable laws : inexorable, regardless Nature. [3]

§ 12. Although God, as the author of Nature, is imagined and represented as a being different from Nature, still what is implied and expressed by this being, its *real contents*, is nothing but Nature. "Ye shall know them by their fruits," we read in the Bible, and the apostle Paul points expressively to the world as to the work wherein God's existence and being can be understood, for what one produces, that contains his being and shows what he is able to do. What we have in Nature, that we have in God, only *imagined as the author or cause of Nature*—therefore no moral and spiritual, but only a natural, physical being. A worship founded only upon God as the author of Nature, without attributing to him any other qualities, derived from man, and without imagining him at the same time as a political and moral, *i. e.* human lawgiver—such worship would be a mere worship of Nature. It is true that the author of Nature is thought to be endowed with intellect and will; but what his will desires, what his intellect thinks, is just that which requires no will nor intellect, but only mechanical, physical, chemical, vegetable and animal forces and impulses.

§ 13. As little as the formation of the child in the womb, the pulsations of the heart, digestion and other organic functions are effects of the intellect and will, so little is Nature in general the effect or production of a spiritual being, *i. e.* of a being that wills and knows or thinks. If Nature was originally a product of the mind, and therefore a manifestation of mind, then also the natural phenomena of the present time would be spiritual effects and manifestations. A supernatural commencement necessarily requires a supernatural continuation. For man thinks intellect and will to be the cause of

Nature only where the effects defy his own will, and surpass his intellect, where he explains things only through human analogies and reasons, where he knows nothing of the natural causes, and therefore derives also the special and present phenomena from God, or—as for instance the movements of the stars which he cannot understand—from subordinate spirits. But if now-a-days the fulcrum of the earth and of the stars is no longer the almighty word of God, and the motive of their movement no spiritual or angelic but a mechanical one: then the first cause of this movement is also necessarily a mechanical, or, in general, a natural one. To derive Nature from intellect and will, or in general from the mind, is to reckon without the host, is *to bring forth the saviour of the world from the virgin without the co-operation of a man, through the Holy Ghost,*—is *to change water into wine,*—is to appease storms *with words*, to transfer mountains *with words*, to restore sight to the blind *with words*. What weakness and narrow-mindedness does it betray to do away with the secondary causes of superstition, such as miracles, devils, spirits etc., in explaining the phenomena of Nature, but to leave untouched the first cause of superstition!

§ 14. Several of the ancient ecclesiastical writers assert, that the Son of God is not a product of God's will, but of God's nature; that the product of Nature is earlier than the product of the will, and that, therefore, the act of begetting, as an act of Nature, precedes the act of creation as an act of the will. Thus the acknowledgment of Nature and her omnipotent laws prevails even within the sphere of the belief in the supernatural God, although in the plainest contradiction of his own will and being. The act of begetting is presupposed to the act of the will; the activity of Nature is considered as preceding the activity of thought and will. This is perfectly true. Nature must necessarily exist before any-thing exists which distinguishes itself from Nature, and which places Nature, as an object of the act of thinking and willing, in opposition to itself. The true way of philosophy leads from the want of intelligence to intel-lect; but the direct way into the madhouse of theology, goes from the intellect to the want of intellect. To base the mind not upon Nature, but, vice versa, Nature upon the mind, is the same as to place the head, not upon the abdomen, but the latter upon the former. Every higher degree of development presupposes the lower one, not vice versa, (⁴) for the simple reason, that the higher one must have something *below* it, in order to be the higher one. And the higher a being stands and the greater its value or dignity is, the more it presupposes. For this very reason not the first being, but the latest, the last, the most depending, the most needful, the most compli-cated being is the highest one, just as in the history of the earth's formation, not the oldest and first works, such as the slate and granite, but the latest and most recent products, such as the basalts and the dense lavas, are the heaviest and weightiest ones. A being which has the honor of presupposing nothing, has also the honor of being nothing. But it is true that the Christians under-stand well the art of making something out of nothing.

§ 15. "All things come from and depend upon God." —so the Christian says in harmony with his godly faith— "but," he adds immediately with his ungodly intellect, "*only indirectly.*" God is only the first cause after which comes the endless host of subordinate Gods, the regiment of intermediate causes. But the intermediate causes, so-called, are the only real and effective ones, the only objective and sensible causes. A God who no longer casts down man with the arrows of Apollo, who no longer arouses the soul with Jove's thunder and lightning, who no longer threatens the sinner with comets and other fiery phenomena, who no longer with his own high hand attracts the iron to the loadstone, produces ebb and tide, and protects the Continent against the overbearing power of the waters which always threaten another deluge—in short, a God driven from the empire of the intermediate causes is only a cause by name, a harmless and very modest creature of imagination—a mere hypothesis for the purpose of solving a theoretical problem, for explaining the commencement of Nature or rather of organic life. For the assumption of a being different from Nature, with the purpose of explaining her existence, has its origin only in the impossibility— although this is only a relative and subjective one—of explaining organic and particularly human life from Nature, inasmuch as the Theist makes his *inability to explain* life through Nature, an *inability of Nature to produce* life out of herself, and thus extends *the limits of his intellect to limits of Nature.*

§ 16. Creation and preservation are inseparable. If, therefore, a being different from Nature—a God—is our creator, he is also our preserver, and not the power of the air, of heat, of the water or of bread, but *the power of God sustains and preserves us.* "In him we live and move and have our being." "Not bread" says Luther, "but *the word of God nourishes also the body* naturally, as it creates and preserves all things." "Because it exists, he (God) nourishes *by it* and *under it*, so that we do not see it, and think that the bread does it. But where it does not exist, he nourishes without the bread, through his word only, as he does it by the bread." "In fine, all creatures are God's masks and mummeries which he permits to assist him in all kind of work that he otherwise can, and really does perform without their co-operation." But if, instead of Nature, God is our preserver, Nature is a mere *disguise* of the Deity, and, therefore, a superfluous and imaginary being, just as vice versa, God is a superfluous and imaginary being if Nature preserves us. But now it is manifest and undeniable that we owe our preservation only to the peculiar effects, qualities and powers of natural beings, therefore we are not only entitled, but compelled, to conclude that we owe also our origin to Nature. We are placed right in the midst of Nature, and should our beginning, our origin, lie outside of Nature? We live within Nature, with Nature, by Nature, and should we still not be of her? What a contradiction!

§ 17. The earth has not always been in its present state, on the contrary, it has come to its actual condition through a series of developments and revolutions, and geology has discovered that in the different stages of its development several species of plants and animals existed, which no longer exist nor even have existed for ages. Thus, for instance, there exist no longer any Trilobites nor any Encinites or Ammonites or Pterodactyles or Ichthyosauri, or Plesiosauri, or Megatheria or Dinotheria, &c. And why not? Apparently because the condition of their existence no longer exist. But if the end of any life coincides with the end of its conditions, then also the beginning, the origin of such life coincides with the origin of its conditions. Even now-a-days where plants, at least those of higher organizations, come to life only by organic procreation, they can—in a very remarkable, yet unexplained manner—be seen to appear in numberless multitudes as soon as the peculiar conditions of their life are given. The origin of organic life cannot, therefore, be thought of as an *isolated* act, as an act *after* the origin of the conditions of life, but rather as the act by which and the moment in which the temperature, the air, the water, the earth in general, received such qualities, and oxygen, hydrogen, carbon, nitrogen entered into such combinations as were necessary for the existence of organic life — this moment must also be considered as the moment when these elements combined for the formation of organic bodies. If, therefore, the earth, by virtue of its own nature, has in the course of time developed and cultivated itself to such a degree that it adopted a character agreeable to the existence of man and suitable to man's nature, or so to say, a *human* character: then it could produce man also by its own power.

§ 18. The power of Nature is not unlimited like the power of God, *i. e.* the power of human imagination ; she cannot do everything at all times and under all circumstances—her productions and effects on the contrary are dependent on conditions. If, therefore, Nature now-a-days cannot or does not produce any organic bodies by *generatio æquivoca*, this is no proof that she could not do it in former times. The present character of the earth is that of stability ; the time of revolutions is gone by, the earth has done raging. The volcanoes only are some single turbulent heads which have no influence on the masses, and which therefore do not disturb the existing order of things. Even the grandest volcanic event within the memory of man, viz., the rising of Jorullo in

Mexico, was nothing but a local rebellion. But as man manifests only in extraordinary times extraordinary powers, or as he can do only in times of the highest exultation and emotion what at other times is impossible for him, and as the plant only at certain epochs, such as the period of germinating, blooming and impregnation produces heat and consumes carbon and hydrogen, thus exhibiting an *animal function*, which is directly in contradiction to its ordinary vegetable functions; so also the earth only in the time of its geological revolutions, when all its powers and elements were in a state of highest fermentation, ebullition and tension, developed its power of producing animals. We know Nature only in its present state; how then could we conclude that what does not happen now by Nature, might not happen at all—even at entirely different times, under entirely different conditions and relations ? [5])

§ 19. The Christians have not been able to express with sufficient strength their astonishment that the heathen adored created beings as divine ones, but they might rather have admired them on that account, for such adoration was based on a perfectly true contemplation of Nature. To be produced, to come into life, is nothing else but to be individualized. All individual beings are produced, but the general fundamental elements or beings of Nature which have no individuality are not produced. Matter is not produced. But an individual being is of a higher, more divine quality than that without individuality. It is true that birth is disgraceful and death painful, but he who does not wish to begin and to end may resign the rank of a living being. Eternity excludes life, and life excludes eternity. Certainly does the individual presuppose another being which pro-

duces it; but the latter does not stand above, it
stands below its product. True, the producing being
is the cause of existence and in that respect the first
being; still it is at the same time the mere means
and material; the basis of another being's existence, and
therefore a subordinate being. The child consumes the
mother, disposes of her strength and of her substance to
his own advantage, paints his cheeks with her blood.
And the child is the mother's pride; she places it above
herself, subordinating her existence and welfare to that
of the child; even the animal mother sacrifices her own
life for that of her young ones. The deepest disgrace of
any being is death, but the source of death is the act of
begetting. To beget is nothing but to throw one's self
away, to make one's self common, to be lost among the
multitude, to sacrifice one's singleness and exclusiveness
to other beings. Nothing is more full of contradiction,
more perverse and void of sense, than to consider the
natural being as produced by a supreme, perfectly spiritual being. According to such a process, and in consis-
tency with the creature's being only an image of the
creator, also the human children ought not to originate
in the disgraceful, lowly placed organ of the womb, but
in the highest organization, the head.

§ 20. The ancient Greeks derived all springs, wells,
streams, lakes and oceans from Oceanos; and the ancient
Persians made all mountains of the earth originate in the
mountain Albordy. Is the derivation of all beings from
one perfect being anything different or better? No, it is
based upon the same manner of thinking. As Albordy
is a mountain like all those which have their origin in it,
so also the divine being, as the source of those derived
from it, is like them, not different from them as to

species; but as the Albordy is distinguished from all
other mountains by preserving their qualities preemin-
ently, *i. e.* in a degree exaggerated by imagination to the
utmost, up to heaven, beyond the sun, moon and stars, so
also the divine being is distinguished from all other beings.
Unity is unproductive; only dualism, contrast, difference
is productive. That which produces the mountains is not
only different from them, but something manifold in
itself. And those elements which produce water, are
not only different from the water, but also from themselves, nay, even antagonistic to one another. Just as
genius, wit, acumen and judgment are produced and developed only by contrasts and conflicts, so also life was
produced only by the conflict of different, nay, of
antagonistic elements, forces and beings.

§ 21. "How should he who made the ear not hear?
How should he who made the eye not see?" This
biblical or theistical derivation of the being endowed
with the senses of hearing and seeing from another being
endowed with the same senses, or to use an expression of
the modern, philosophic language, the derivation of the
spiritual and subjective being from another spiritual and
subjective being, is based upon the same foundation, and
expresses the same as the biblical explanation of the
rain from heavenly masses of water collected beyond or
in the clouds, or the Persian derivation of the mountains
from the original mountain, Albordy, or the Grecian explanation of fountains and rivers from Oceanos. Water
from water, but from an immensely great and all-embracing water; mountain from mountain, but from an infinite
all-embracing mountain; so spirit from spirit, life from
life, eye from eye—but from an infinite, all-embracing
eye, life and spirit.

§ 22. When children inquire about the origin of babes, we give them the *explanation* that the nurse takes them from the well where they swim like fishes. The explanation which theology gives us of the origin of organic or natural beings in general is not much different. God is the deep or beautiful well of imagination in which all realities, all perfections, all forces are contained, in which all things swim already made like little fishes. Theology is the nurse who takes them from this well, but the chief person, Nature, the mother who brings forth the children with pangs, who bears them during nine months under her heart, is left entirely out of consideration in such an explanation, which originally was only childlike, but now-a-days is childish. Certainly such an explanation is more beautiful, more pleasant to the heart, easier, more intelligible and conceivable to the children of God than the natural way, which only by degrees and through numberless obstacles rises from darkness to light. But also the explanation which our pious forefathers gave of hailstorms, epidemics among cattle, drought and thunderstorms, by tracing them to the agency of weather-makers, sorcerers, and witches, is far more practical, easier, and, to uneducated men even now-a-days much more intelligible than the explanation of these phenomena from natural causes.

§ 23. "The origin of life is inexplicable and inconceivable." Be it so; but this incomprehensibility does not justify us in drawing from it the superstitious consequences which theology draws from the deficiencies of human knowledge, nor in going beyond the sphere of natural causes: for we can only say, "we cannot explain life from these natural phenomena and causes which are known to us, or *as far* as they are known to us"—but we cannot say, "life cannot be explained at all from Nature," without pretending to have exhausted already the ocean of Nature even to the last drop. This incomprehensibility does not justify us in explaining the inexplicable by the supposition of *imagined* beings, and in deceiving and deluding ourselves and others by an explanation which explains nothing. It does not justify us in changing an ignorance of natural material causes into a non-existence of such causes, and in deifying, personifying, representing our ignorance in a being which is to destroy such ignorance, and which yet does not express anything but the nature of such ignorance, the deficiency of positive, material reasons of explanation. For what else is the immaterial, incorporeal, not natural, extramundane being to whom we thus try to trace back all life, but the precise expression of the intellectual absense of material, corporeal, natural, cosmical causes? But instead of being so honest and modest as to say frankly: "We do not know any reason, we do not know how to explain it, we have no data nor materials," you change these deficiencies, these negations, these vacancies of your head by the activity of your imagination into positive beings, into immaterial beings, *i. e.* into beings which are not material nor natural, because you do not know of any material or natural causes. While ignorance however is contented with immaterial, incorporeal, unnatural beings, her inseparable companion, wanton imagination, which always and exclusively indulges in the intercourse with beings of the highest perfection, immediately elevates these poor creatures of ignorance to the rank of supermaterial, supernatural beings.

§ 24. The idea that Nature or the universe in general

has a real beginning, and that consequently at sometime there was no Nature, no universe, is a narrow idea, which seems acceptable to man only as long as he has a narrow, limited conception of the world. It is an imagination without sense and foundation—this imagination that at some time nothing real existed, for the universe is the totality of all reality. All qualities or definitions of God which make him an objective, real being are only qualities *abstracted from Nature*, which presuppose and define Nature, and which therefore would not exist if Nature did not exist. It is true, if we abstract from Nature : if in our thoughts or our imagination we destroy her existence, *i. e.* if we shut our eyes and extinguish all images of natural things reflected by our senses and conceive Nature not with our senses (not *in concreto* as the philosophers say) there is left a being, a totality of qualities such as infinity, power, unity, necessity, eternity ; but this being which is left after deducting all qualities and phenomena reflected by our senses is in truth nothing but the abstract essence of Nature, or Nature "*in abstract,*" in thought. And such derivation of Nature or the universe from God is therefore in this respect nothing but the derivation of the real essence of Nature, as it appears to our senses, from her abstract, imagined essence, which exists only in our idea—a derivation which appears to be reasonable because in the act of thinking we are accustomed to consider the abstract and general as that which is nearer to thought, and which therefore must be presupposed to the individual, the real, the concrete, as that which is higher and earlier in thought, although in reality just the reverse takes place, inasmuch as Nature exists before God, *i. e.* the concrete before the abstract that which we conceive with our senses before that which is thought. In reality, where everything passes on naturally, the copy follows the original, the image the thing which it represents, the thought its object— but on the supernatural, miraculous ground of theology, the original follows the copy, the thing its own likeness. " It is strange " says St. Augustine, " but nevertheless true, that this world could not exist if it was not known to God." That means: the world is known and thought before it exists; nay, it *exists* only *because* it was thought of—the existence is a consequence of the knowledge or of the act of thinking, the original a consequence of the copy, the object a consequence of its likeness.

§ 25. If we reduce the world or Nature to a totality of abstract qualities, to a metaphysical, *i. e.* to a merely imagined object, and consider this abstract world as the real world, then it is a logical necessity to consider it as finite. The world is not given to us through the act of thinking, not at least through the metaphysical and hyperphysical thinking which abstracts from the real world and founds its true and highest existence upon such abstraction—the world is given to us through life, by perception, by the senses. For an abstract being which only thinks there exists no light, because it has no eyes, no warmth, because it has no feeling, in general no world because it has no organ for its perception; for such a being there exists in reality *nothing*. The world, therefore, exists for us only because we are no logical or metaphysical beings, because we are other beings, because we are more than mere logicians and metaphysicians. But just this *plus* appears to the metaphysical thinker as a *minus*, this negation of the art of thinking as an absolute negation. Nature to him is nothing but the opposite of mind. This merely negative and abstract definition he makes her positive definition, her essence. Consequently it is a contradiction to consider as a positive being that being, or rather that nonentity which is only the negation of the act of thinking, which is an imagined thing, but according to its nature an object of the senses, that is antagonistic to the act of thinking and to the mind. The being which exists in thought is for the thinker the true essence, therefore it is self-evident to him that a being which does not exist in thought cannot be a true, eternal, original essence. It implies already a contradiction for the mind to think only of its opposite ; it is only in harmony with itself when it thinks only itself (on the standpoint of metaphysical speculation,) or at least (on the standpoint of theism) when it thinks an essence which expresses nothing but the nature of the act of thinking, which is given only by thought, and which therefore in itself is nothing but an imagined being. Thus Nature disappears into nothing. But still she *exists*, though according to the thinker she neither can nor should be. How then does the metaphysician explain her existence ? By a self-privation, a self-negation, a self-denial of the mind which apparently is a voluntary one, but which in very truth is contradictory to, and only enforced upon his inner nature. But if Nature on the standpoint of abstract thinking disappears into nothing, on the other hand on the standpoint of the real observation and contemplation of the world, that creative mind disappears into nothing. On this standpoint all deductions of the world from God, of Nature from the mind, of physics from metaphysics, of the real from the abstract, are proved to be nothing but *logical plays*.

§ 26. Nature is the first and fundamental object of
religion, but she is such an object even where she is the
direct and immediate object of religious adoration, as *e.
g.* in the natural religions so-called, not as such, as
Nature, i. e., in the manner and in the sense in which
we regard her from the standpoint of theism or of
philosophy and of the natural sciences. Nature is to
man originally, i. e., where he regards her with a religious eye, rather an object of his own qualities, a personal, living, feeling being. Man originally does not distinguish himself from Nature, nor consequently Nature
from himself, therefore the sensations which any object
in Nature excites in him appear to him immediately as
qualities of the object. The beneficial, good sensations
and effects are caused by good and benevolent Nature,
the bad, painful sensations, such as heat, cold, hunger,
pain, disease, by an evil being, or at least by Nature in a
state of evil disposition, of malevolence, of wrath. Thus
man involuntarily and unconsciously, *i. e.*, necessarily—
although this necessity is only a relative and historical
one—transforms the essence of Nature into a feeling,
i. e. a subjective, a human being. No wonder that he
then also expressively, knowingly and willingly transforms her into an object of religion, of prayer, *i. e.* an
object which can be influenced by the feelings of man,
his prayers, his services. Really, man has made Nature
already subservient and subdued her to himself by
assimilating her to his feelings and subduing her to his
passions. Besides, uneducated natural man does not
only presuppose human motives, impulses and passions
in Nature, he sees even real men in natural bodies.
Thus the Indians on the Orinoco think the sun, the moon
and the stars, to be men—" those up there," they say " are

men like unto us;" The Patagonians think the stars to be "former Indians;" the Greenlanders think the sun, moon and stars, to be their ancestors, who at a particular occasion were translated into heaven." Thus also the ancient Mexicans believed that the sun and the moon which they adored as gods had been men in former times. Behold thus the assertion made in my "Essence of Christianity" that man in religion is in relation to an intercourse with himself only, and that his God in reality reflects only his own essence—this assertion is confirmed even by the most uncultivated, primary manifestations of religion ; where man adores things the most distant from and most unlike to himself, such as stars, stones, trees, nay, even the claws of crabs, and snail shells ; for he adores them only because he transfers himself into them, because he believes them to be such beings, or at least to he inhabited by such beings as himself. Religion therefore exhibits the remarkable contradiction, which however is easily understood, nay, even necessary, that, while on one hand (from the standpoint of theism or anthropologism) she worships the human essence as a divine one, because it appears to her as different from man, as an essence not human—on the other hand (from the materialistic standpoint) she adores *vice versa* the essence which is not human as a divine one, because it appears to her as a human one.

§ 27. The mutability of Nature, especially in those phenomena which most of all cause man to feel his dependence on her, is the principal reason why she appears to man as a human, arbitrary being, and why she is religiously adored by him. If the sun stood always in the sky, he would never have kindled the fire of religious passion in man. Only when he disappeared from man's

eye and inflicted upon him the terrors of night, and when
again he re-appeared, man fell down on his knees before
him, overcome by joy at his unexpected return. Thus
the ancient Apalachites in Florida greeted the sun with
hymns at his rising and setting, and prayed to him at
the same time that he might return and bless them with
his light. If the earth always produced fruits, where
would there be a motive for religious celebrations of the
time of sowing and harvesting? Only in consequence of
her now opening, now closing her womb, her fruits appear to be her *voluntary* gifts which oblige man to be
grateful. The changes in Nature make man uncertain,
humble, religious. It is uncertain, whether the weather
to-morrow will be favorable to my undertakings; is it
uncertain whether I shall harvest what I sow, and therefore I cannot depend upon the gifts of Nature as upon a
tribute due, or an infallible consequence. But where
mathematical certainty is at an end, there theology
commences, even now-a-days in weak minds. Religion
is the conception of the necessary—or of the accidental
—as of something arbitrary, or voluntary. The opposite
sentiment, that of irreligion and ungodliness, on the
other hand, is represented by the Cyclops of Euripides,
when he says: "Earth must produce grass for feeding
my flock, *whether she be willing to do so or not.*"

§ 28. The feeling of dependence upon Nature in
combination with the imagination of her as of an arbitrarily acting, personal being, is the motive of the *sacrifice,* the most essential act of natural religion. The dependence upon Nature is particularly sensible to me by my
want of her. The want is the feeling and expression of
my nothingness without Nature; but inseparable from
want is enjoyment, the opposite feeling, the feeling of

my self-existence, of my independence in distinction from Nature. Want, therefore, is pious, humble, religious—but enjoyment is haughty, ungodly, void of respect, frivolous. And such frivolity, or at least want of respect in enjoyment, is a practical necessity for man, a necessity upon which his existence is founded—but a necessity which is in direct contradiction to his theoretical respect for Nature as for an egotistic, sensible being, which suffers as little as man that anything be taken from her. The appropriation or the use of Nature appears therefore to man, as if it were an encroachment upon her right, as an appropriation of another one's property, as an outrage. In order now to propitiate his conscience as well as the object of his imaginary offence; in order to show that his robbery has its origin in want, not in arrogance, he diminishes his enjoyment and returns to the object a part of its plundered property. Thus the Greeks believed that if a tree were cut down, its soul, the Dryad, lamented and cried to Fate for revenge against the trespasser. Thus no Roman ventured to cut down a tree on his ground without sacrificing a farrow for the propitiation of the god or goddess of this grove. Thus the Ostiaks, after having slain a bear, suspend its skin on a tree, pay to it all sorts of reverences, and apologize as well as they can to the bear for having killed him. "They believe in this manner politely to avert the damage which the spirit of the animal possibly could inflict upon them." Thus North American tribes by similar ceremonies propitiate the departed souls of slain beasts. Thus the Philippines asked the plains and mountains for their permission, if they wished to cross them, and deemed it a crime to cut down any old tree. And the Bramin hardly dares to drink water or to tread upon the ground with his feet, because each step, each draught of water causes pain and death to sentient beings, plants as well as animals, and he must therefore do penance "in order to atone for the death of creatures which he possibly, although unconsciously might destroy by day or night." ([6])

§ 29.   The sacrifice makes perceptible to the senses the whole essence of religion.   Its source is the feeling of dependence, fear, doubt, the uncertainty of success, of future events, the scruples of conscience on account of a sin committed; but the result, the purpose of the sacrifice is self-consciousness, courage, enjoyment, the certainty of success, liberty and happiness.   As a servant of Nature I observe the sacrifice; as her master I depart from it.   Therefore, although the feeling of dependence upon Nature is the source and motive of religion: its very purpose and end is the destruction of such feeling, the independence from Nature.   Or, although the divinity of Nature is the basis, the foundation of religion generally and of Christian religion in particular, still its end is the divinity of man.

§ 30.   Religion has for its presupposition the contradiction between *will* and *ability*, desire and satisfaction, intention and success, imagination and reality, thought and existence.   In his desire, in his imagination, man is unlimited, free, almighty—God; but in his ability, in reality, he is bound, dependent, limited—*man*; man in the sense of a finite being, in contradistinction from God. "Man proposes, God disposes," as the saying is.   "Man plans and Jove accomplishes it differently."   The thought, the will is *mine*; but what I think and will is *not* mine, is outside of me, does not depend on me.   The destruction of such a contrast or contradiction is the tendency, the purpose of religion; and that being in which

it is destroyed, and wherein that which I wish and imagine as possible, which however my limited power proves
to be impossible for me, is possible, nay even real—that
being is the divine being.

§ 31. That which is independent from the will and
the knowledge of man is the original, proper, character-
istic cause of religion—the cause of God. "I have
planted" says Paul, "Apollos watered, but God gave
the increase. So then neither is he that planteth anything, neither he that watereth, but God that giveth the
increase." And Luther says: "We must praise and
thank God that he suffers grain to grow, and acknowledge that it is not our work, but his blessing and his
gift, if grain and wine and all sorts of fruit grow which
we eat and drink to satisfy our wants." And Hesiod
says, that the industrious husbandman will richly harvest
if Jove grants a good end. The tilling of the soil then,
the sowing and watering of the seed, depends on me, but
not the succes. This is in God's hand, therefore it is
said: "God's blessing is the main thing." But what is
God? originally nothing but Nature, or the essence of
Nature; but Nature as an object of prayer, as an exor-
able and consequently willing being. Jove is the cause
or the essence of meteorological phenomena; but this
does not yet constitute his divine, his religious character; also he who is not religious assumes a cause of the
rain, of the thunder storm, of the snow. He is God
only, because and in so far as these phenomena depend on his good will. That which is independent
of man's will is, therefore, by religion, made dependent upon God's will as far as the object itself is concerned (objectively); but subjectively (as far as man is
concerned,) it is made dependent on prayer, for what

depends on will is an object of prayer and can be
changed. "*Even the Gods are pliable.* A mortal can
change their minds by incense and humble vows, by li-
bations and perfume."

§ 32. The only or at least the principal object of religion is an object of human purposes and wants, at least
where man has once risen beyond the unlimited arbitrariness, helplessness and accidentalness of Fetishism
proper. For this very reason those natural beings which
are most necessary and indispensable to man enjoyed also the most general and the highest religious adoration.
But whatever is an object of human wants and purposes,
is for the same reason an object of *human wishes.* I
need rain and sunshine for the successful growth of my
seeds. In times of continuous drouth I therefore wish
for rain; in times of continuous rain I wish for sunshine.
This wish is a desire whose gratification is not within my
power; a will, but without the might to prevail, although
not absolutely so, yet at least at a given time, under certain circumstances and conditions, and such as man
wishes it on the stand point of religion. But just what
my body, my power in general, is unable to do, is within
the power of my wish. What I ask and wish for, that I
enchant and inspire by my wishes. ([7]) While under the
influence of an affect—and religion roots only in affect,
in feeling—man places his essence without himself; he
treats as living what is without life, as arbitrary what
has no will; he animates the object with his sighs, for he
cannot possibly in a state of affect address himself to an
insensible being. Feeling does not confine itself within
the limits prescribed by intellect; it gushes over man;
his breast is too narrow for it; it must communicate itself to the outer world and by so doing make the insensi-

ble essence of Nature a sympathetic one. Nature enchanted by human feeling, Nature agreeing with and assimilated to man's feeling, *i. e.*, Nature herself endowed with feeling, is Nature *such as she is an object of religion, a divine being.* The wish is the *origin; the very essence of religion—the essence of the Gods is nothing but the essence of the wish.* (⁸) The Gods are superhuman and supernatural beings; but are not wishes also of a *superhuman* and *supernatural* nature ? *e. g.* am I in my wish, in my imagination still a man, if I wish to be an immortal being, free from the fetters of the earthly body ? No ! He who has no wishes has no gods either. Why did the Greeks lay such a stress upon the immortality and happiness of the Gods ? Because they themselves did not wish to be mortal and unhappy. Where no lamentations about man's mortality and misery are heard, no hymns are heard in honor of the immortal and happy Gods. Only the water of tears shed within the human heart evaporates in the sky of imaginatian into the cloudy image of the divine being. From the universal stream, Oceanos, Homer derives the Gods ; but this stream abounding with Gods *is in reality* only an efflux of human feelings.

§ 33. The irreligious manifestations of religion are best adapted to disclose in a popular manner the origin and essence of religion. Thus it is an irreligious manifestation of religion and therefore most severely criticized already by the pious heathen, that as a general thing man takes recourse to religion, that he applies to God and thinks of him, only in times of misfortune ; but this very fact reveals to us the source of religion. In times of misfortune or distress, no matter whether it be his own or another one's, man realizes the painful experience

of his inability to do what he wishes—he finds his hands
tied.   But the palsy of the motory nerves is not at the
same time also the palsy of the sensory nerves; the fetters
of my physical power are not also at the same time the
fetters of my will, of my heart.   On the contrary, the
more my hands are tied, the more boundless are my
wishes, the more ardent is my desire for redemption, the
more energetic my strife after freedom, my will not to
be limited.   The power of the human heart or will which
by the influence of distress has been exaggerated and
overexcited to a superhuman one, is the power of the
Gods for whom there is no necessity nor limit.   The
Gods are able to do what man desires, *i. e.* they obey
the laws of the human heart.   What man is only in regard to his soul, the Gods are also physically; what he
can do only within his will, his imagination, his heart, *i.
e.*, *mentally*, as *e. g.* to be in the twinkling of an eye at
a distant place, *that* the Gods are able to do *physically.*
The Gods are the embodied, realized wishes of man—
the natural limits of man's heart and will destroyed—
creatures of the unlimited will, creatures whose physical
powers are equal to those of the will.   The irreligious
manifestation of this supernatural power of religion is
the *practice of witchcraft* among uncivilized nations,
where in a *palpable* manner the *mere will* of man appears as God, commanding over Nature.   But when the
God of Israel at Joshua's command bids the sun stand
still or suffers it to rain in compliance with Elijah's
prayer, and when the God of the Christians for the sake
of proving his divinity, *i. e.*, his power to fulfill all wishes
of man, by his word alone appeases the raging sea, cures
the sick, raises the dead : here as well as in the practice
of witchcraft, the mere will, the mere wish, the mere

word is declared a power that overrules Nature. The only difference is that the sorcerer realizes the end of religion in an irreligious manner, whilst the Jew and the Christians do it in a religious manner, inasmuch as the former places *within himself*, what the latter transfers *into God*, inasmuch as the former makes the object of an expressive will or command what the latter make the object of a *still* submissive will, of a pious wish; in short inasmuch as the former does by and for himself, what the latter do by and with God. But the common saying: "*quod quis per alium fecit ipse fecisse putatur,*" *i. e.* what one does through another one that is imputed to him as his own deed, finds its application also here: what one does *through God*, that he does *in reality himself*.

§ 34. Religion has—at least originally and in relation to nature—no other office and tendency than to change the unpopular and haunted essence of Nature into a familiar and known one; to melt Nature, who in herself is impliant and hard as iron, in the glowing fire of the heart for the sake of human purposes; *i. e.*, it has the same end as civilization or culture, whose end also is no other than to make Nature theoretically an intelligible and practically a pliable being, agreeable to the wants of man—*with this only difference*, that what culture tries to attain *by means*, and that too by means learned from Nature, religion attains without means, or what is the same, through the supernatural means of prayer, of faith, of sacraments, of witchcraft. Thus we find that everything which with the progress of the civilization of mankind became a cause of activity, of self-activity, of *anthropology*, in former times was a cause of *religion* or *theology;* as, for instance, jurisprudence, politics, medicine, which latter even now-a-days among uncivilized nations is a thing of religion.([9]) It is true, culture and civilization always come short of the wishes of religion, for it cannot destroy those limits of man which have their foundation in his Nature. Thus culture succeeds for instance in improving the science of prolonging life (Macrobiotics) but it never attains to immortality. This as a boundless wish which cannot be realized is left to religion.

§ 35. In natural religion man addresses himself to an object directly antagonistic to the original will and sense of religion; for here he sacrifices his feelings and his intellect to a being which in itself is without feeling and intellect; he places above himself what he would like to have below himself; he serves what he wishes to govern, adores what in reality he abhors, entreats for assistance that against which he seeks assistance. Thus the Greeks at Titane sacrificed to the winds in order to appease their rage; thus the Romans dedicated a temple to the Fever in order to render it harmless; thus the Tungusians at the time of an epidemic pray devotionally and with solemn bows to *the disease that it may pass by their huts* (according to Pallas.) Thus the Widahians in Guinea sacrifice to the raging sea in order to prevail upon it that it may be calm and not prevent them from fishing; thus the Indians at the approach of a storm address the Manitou (*i. e.* Spirit, God, Being) of the air, at the crossing of water the Manitou of the waters, that he may preserve them from all danger; thus in general many nations expressively do not adore the good but the evil essence ([10]) of Nature, or at least what appears *to them as such*. Upon the standpoint of natural religion man declares his love to a statue, to a corpse; no wonder therefore, that in order to make himself heard he resorts to the most desperate, most insane means; no wonder that he *divests himself of his humanity in order to render Nature humane,* that he even *sheds the blood of man* in order to *inspire her with human feelings.* Thus the northern Germans believed expressly that " *sanguinary sacrifices* were apt to bestow *human language and feelings to wooden idols* and to endow with the gifts of *language* and divination the *stones* which they adored in the houses devoted to gory sacrifices." But in vain are all attempts to imbue her with life ; Nature does not respond to man's lamentations and questions ; she throws him inexorably back upon himself.

§ 36. As the limits which man imagines or at least such as he imagines them on the standpoint of religion (as *e. g.* the limit which is the cause that he does not know the future, or does not live forever, or does not enjoy happiness without interruption and molestation, or has no body without weight, or cannot fly like the Gods, or cannot thunder like Jove, or cannot add anything to his size nor make himself invisible at will, or cannot, like the angels, live without sensual wants and impulses, or in short cannot do what he wills and desires)—as all these limits are such only in his imagination and mind, while in reality they are no limits, because they have their *necessary* foundation in the *essence,* in the *nature* of things; so also is that being which is free from such limits, the unlimited divine being, only a creature of imagination, of reflection, and of a mental disposition which is governed by imagination. Whatever therefore may be the object of religion, be it even only a snail shell or pebble, it is such an object only in its quality *as a creature of the heart, of reflection, of imagination.*

This justifies the assertion that men do not adore the stones, the trees, the animals, the rivers themselves, but the Gods within them, their manitous, their spirits. But these spirits of natural objects are nothing but *their reflected images* or *they as reflected objects*, as *creatures of imagination in distinction from them as real, sensual objects*, just as the spirits of the dead are nothing but the imagined images of the dead which live in our remembrance—*beings that once really existed, as imagined beings*, which however by religious man, *i. e.* by him who does not discriminate between the object and its idea, are considered to be real, self-existing beings. Man's pious, involuntary self-deception upon the standpoint of religion is therefore within the natural religion an *apparent, self-evident truth;* for here man gives to his religious object eyes and ears which he knows and sees to be *artificial* eyes and ears of *s   e* or *wood*, and yet *believes* to be *real* eyes and ears. Thus religious man has his eyes only in order *not* to see, to be stone-blind, and his reason only in order *not* to reason, to be block-headed. Natural religion is the manifest contradiction between idea and reality, between imagination and truth. What in reality is a dead stone or log, is in the conception of natural religion a living individual; *apparently, no* God, but something entirely different, yet *invisibly*, according to belief, a *God*. For this reason, natural religion is always in danger of being most bitterly undeceived, as it requires only a blow with an axe in order to satisfy her, *e. g.* that no blood flows from adored trees, and that therefore no living, divine being dwells within them. But how does religion escape these strong contradictions and disappointments to which she is exposed by adoring Nature? Only by making her object *an invisible, not sensual* one, by making it a being that exists *only* in faith, reflection, imagination—in short, within the mind, which therefore itself is a spiritual being.

§ 37. As soon as man from a merely physical being becomes a political one, or in general a being distinguishing himself from Nature, and concentrating himself within himself, his God is also changed from a merely physical being into a *political* one, *different from Nature.* That which leads man to a distinction of his essence from Nature, and in consequence to a God distinguished from Nature, is therefore only his association with other men to a *commonwealth*, wherein the objects of his consciousness and of his *feeling of dependence* are powers distinguished from those of Nature and existing only in thought or imagination; political, moral, abstract powers, such as the power of law, of public opinion, (¹¹) of honor, of virtue—while his physical existence is subordinated to his human, political or moral existence, and where the power of Nature, the power over death and life, is degraded to an attribute and instrument of political or moral power. Jove is the God of lightning and thunder; but he possesses these terrible weapons only in order to crush those who disobey his commandments, the perjurer, the perpetrators of violence. Jove is father of the kings—"from Jove are the kings."

With lightning and thunder therefore Jove sustains the power and dignity of the Kings. (¹²) "The King," we read in the law-book of Menu, "*burns eyes and hearts like the sun*, therefore no human creature upon earth is able even to look upon him. *He is fire and air, he is sun and moon*, he is the God of criminal laws.

Fire burns only a single one who by carelessness may have approached too near to it, but a King's fire when he is in wrath, burns a whole family with all their cattle and property — — — — — In his courage dwelleth conquest and *death in his wrath*." In a similar manner the God of the Israelites commands amid lightning and thunder his people to walk in all ways which he has commanded them "in order that they may prosper and live long in the land." Thus the power of Nature as such and the feeling of dependence on her disappears before political or moral power! Whilst the slave of Nature is so blinded by the brilliancy of the sun, that he like the Katchinian Tartar daily prays to him: "do not kill me," the political slave on the other hand is so much blinded by the splendor of royal dignity, that he prostrates himself before it as before a divine power; because it commands over death and life. The titles of the Roman Emperors, even still among the Christians were: "Your divinity," "Your eternity." Nay, even now-a-days among Christians "Holiness" and "Majesty," the titles and attributes of the Deity, are titles and attributes of kings. It is true the Christians try to justify this political idolatry with the notion that the king is nothing but God's representative upon earth, God himself being the King of kings. But such a justification is only a self-deception. Not considering that the king's power is a very sensible, direct and sensual one which represents itself, while that of the King of kings is only an indirect and reflected one—God is defined and regarded as the world's ruler, as a royal or political being in general, only where the royal being occupies, influences and rules man so as to be considered by him as the *supreme being*. "Brahma" says Menu, "formed in the beginning of time

for his service the *genius of punishment* with a body of
pure light as *his own son*, nay even as the author or
criminal justice, as the *protector of all things created.*
Fear of punishment enables this universe to enjoy its
happiness." Thus man makes even the punishment of
his criminal code divine, world-governing powers, the
criminal code itself the code of Nature, no wonder that
he makes Nature to sympathize most warmly with his
political sufferings and passions, nay, that he even makes
the preservation of the world dependent on the preservation of a royal throne or of the Holy See. What is important to him, naturally is also of importance for all
other beings ; what dims his eye, that also dims the brilliancy of the sun; what agitates his heart, that also
moves heaven and earth—his being to him is the universal being, the world's being, the being of beings.

§ 38. Why has the East not a living, progressive
history such as the West? Because in the East to man
Nature is not concealed by man, nor the brilliancy of
the stars and precious stones by the brilliancy of the eye,
nor the meteorological lightning and thunder by the
rhetorical "lightning and thunder," nor the course of
the sun by the course of daily events, nor the change of
the year's seasons by the change of fashion. It is true,
the eastern man prostrates himself into the dust before
the magnificence of royal, political power and dignity,
but this magnificence itself is only a reflex of the sun and
the moon; the king is an object of his adoration not as
an earthly and human, but as a heavenly and divine
being. But man disappears by the side of a God ; only
where the earth is depopulated of Gods, where the Gods
ascend into heaven and change from real beings to imagined ones; only there men have space and room for

themselves, only there they can show themselves without
any restraint as men and put themselves forward as such.
The eastern man bears the same relation to the western
man as the husbandman to the inhabitants of the city.
The former depends on Nature, the latter on man; the
former is led by the barometer, the latter by the state
of the stock-market; the former by the ever equal con-
stellations of the zodiac, the latter by the ever fluctuating
signs of honor, fashion and public opinion. Only the
inhabitants of cities, therefore, make up history, only
human "vanity" is the principle of history, only he who
can sacrifice Nature's power to that of opinion, his life
to his name, his physical existence to his existence in
the mouth and in the remembrance of generations to
come—he only is capable of historical deeds.

§ 39. According to Athenæus, the Greek writer of
comic plays, Anaxandrides addresses the Egyptians as
follows: "I am not fit for your society; our manners
and laws do not agree,—you adore the ox which I sacrifice to the Gods; the eel to you is a great God, but to
me a great dainty; you shun pork, I enjoy it with a
relish; you revere the dog, I beat him if he snaps a
morsel from me; you are startled if something is the
matter with the cat, I am glad of it and strip off her skin;
you give a great deal of importance to the shrew-mouse,
I none." This address perfectly characterizes the contrast between the bound and the unbound, *i. e.* between
the religious and irreligious, free, human consideration of
Nature. There Nature is an object of adoration, here
of enjoyment; there man exists for Nature's sake, here
Nature for man's sake, there she is the end, here the
means; there she stands above, here below man.([13]) For
this very reason man is there eccentric, out of himself out

of the sphere of his destination which points him only to himself; here, on the other hand, he is considerate, sober, within himself, self-conscious. There man degrades himself consistently even to coition with animals (according to Herodotus), in order to prove his religious humility before Nature; but here he rises in the full consciousness of his power and dignity up to amalgamation with the Gods as a striking proof that even in the heavenly Gods courses no other than human blood, and that the peculiar ethereal blood of the Gods is only a poetical imagination which does not hold good in reality and practice.

§ 40. As the world, as Nature *appears* to man, so she *is i e.* for him, according to his imagination; his sensations and imaginations are to him directly and unconsciously the measure of truth and reality; and Nature *appears to him just as he is himself.* As soon as man perceives that in spite of sun and moon, heaven and earth, fire and water, plants and animals, man's life requires the application and even the just application of his own powers; as soon as he perceives that "the mortals unjustly complain of the Gods, and that *they themselves in spite of fate, through imprudence, produce their misery,*" that the consequences of vice and folly are disease, unhappiness and death, but those of virtue and wisdom, health, life and happiness, and that, therefore, those powers which influence man's destiny, are intellect and will; as soon, therefore, as man no more like the savage, is a being governed by the habits of momentary impressions and effects, but becomes a being which decides himself by principles, rules of wisdom, laws of reason, *i. e. a* thinking, intelligent being—then also Nature, *the world,* appears and is to him a *being dependent on, and influenced by, intellect and will.*

§ 41. When man with his will and intellect rises above Nature and becomes a supernaturalist, then also God becomes a supernatural being. When man establishes himself as a ruler "over the fishes in the sea, and over the fowl of the air, and over the cattle, and over all the earth, and over every creeping thing that creepeth over the earth," then the Government of Nature is to him the *highest idea*, the *highest being ;* the object of his adoration, of his religion therefore, the creator of Nature, for creation is a necessary consequence, or rather presupposition, of Government. If the Lord of Nature is not also her author, then she is independent of him as to her origin and existence, his power is limited and deficient ;—for if he *had been able* to create her, why should he not have created her ?—his government is only an *usurped* one, no inherent, legal one. Only what I produce and make is entirely within my power. Only from authorship the right of property is to be derived. Mine is the child, because I am his father. Therefore, only in creation government is acknowledged, realized, exhausted. The Gods of the heathen were also already masters of Nature, it is true, but no creators of hers, therefore they were only constitutional, limited, not *absolute monarchs* of Nature, *i. e. the heathen were not yet absolute, unconditional, radical supernaturalists.*

§ 42. The Theists have declared the doctrine of the unity of God a revealed doctrine of supernatural origin, without considering that the source of Monotheism is in man, that the scource of God's unity is the unity of the human conscience and mind. The world is spread before my eyes in endless multitude and diversity, but still all these numberless and various objects : sun, moon and stars, heaven and earth, the near and the distant, the present and the absent, are embraced by my mind, my head. This being of the human mind or conscience, so wonderful and supernatural for religious, *i. e.* uneducated man, this being which is not restrained by any limits of time or space, which is not limited to any particular species of things, and which embraces all things and beings, without being himself an object or visible being—this being is, by Monotheism, placed at the head of the world, and made its *cause*. God *speaks*, God *thinks the world* and *it is*, he says that it is not, he thinks and wills it not, and it does not exist, *i. e.* I can in my imagination cause at will all things and consequently also the world itself to come and to disappear, to originate and to pass away. That God has also created the world from nothing, and, if he will, thrusts it again into nothing, is nothing but the personification of the *human power of abstraction and imagination,* which enables me at will to imagine the world as existing or not existing, and to affirm or deny its existence. This *subjective* or *imagined non-existence* of the world, is by Monotheism made its *objective*, real *non-existence*. Polytheism and natural religion in general make the real objects imagined ones. Monotheism, on the other hand, makes imagined objects and thoughts real objects, or rather the essence of intellect, will and imagination the most real, absolute, supreme being. The power of God, says a theologian, extends as far as the imaginative power of man, but where is the limit of this power? What is impossible to imagination? I can imagine everything that is, as not existing, and everything that does not exist as real; thus I can imagine "this" world as not existing, and on the other hand, numberless other worlds as existing. What is imagined as real is possible.

But God is the being to whom *nothing is impossible*, he is the creator of numberless worlds, as far as his power is concerned, the *possibility of all possibilities, of everything that can be imagined; i. e.* in reality, he is nothing but the realization or personification of human imagination, intellect and reflection, thought or imagined as real, nay, as the most real, as the absolute being.

§ 43. Theism, properly so-called, or Monotheism, arises only where man refers Nature only *to himself*, because she suffers herself to be used *without will* and *consciousness*, not only to his necessary, organic functions, but also to his *arbitrary, conscious* purposes and enjoyments, and where he makes *this relation her essence*, consequently making himself the purpose, the *centre* and *unity* of Nature. (¹⁴) Where Nature has *her end outside of herself*, she necessarily has also her *cause* and *beginning without herself;* where she exists *only for another being*, she necessarily exists also *by another being*, and that by a being whose intention or end at the time of her creation was man, as that being who was to enjoy and to use Nature for his good. The *beginning* of Nature coincides therefore with *God* only where her *end* coincides with *man*, or in other words, the doctrine that God is the *creator of the world* has its *source* and *sense* in the doctrine that man is the *end* of creation. If you feel ashamed of the belief that the world is created, *made* for man, then you must feel ashamed of the belief that it is *created, made at all.* Where it is written: "In the beginning God created the heaven and the earth," there it is also written: "God made two great lights. He made the stars also, and set them in the firmament of the heaven, to give *light upon the earth, and to rule over the day and the night.*" If you declare the belief in man as the end of Nature to be human pride, then you must also declare *the belief in the creator of Nature to be human pride.* That light only which shines on account of man is the light of theology, that light only which exists exclusively on account of the seeing being, presupposes also a seeing being as its cause.

§ 44. The spiritual being. which man places above Nature and presupposes as her founder and creator, is nothing but the *spiritual essence of man himself,* which, however, appears to him as *another* one, *different* from and *incomparable* to himself, because he makes it the *cause of Nature,* the cause of effects which man's mind, will and intellect cannot produce, and because he consequently combines with that spiritual essence of man, *the essence of Nature which is different.* (¹⁵) It is the divine spirit who makes the grass grow, who forms the child in the womb, who holds and moves the sun in his course, who piles up the mountains, commands the winds, incloses the sea within its limits. What is the human mind compared with this spirit ! How small, how limited, how vain ! If therefore the rationalist rejects God's incarnation, the union of the divine and human nature, he does so particularly because the idea of God in his head *hides* only the idea of Nature, especially of Nature such as she was disclosed to the human eye by the telescope of astronomy. How should—thus he exclaims provoked—how should that great, infinite, universal being, which has its adequate representation and effect only in the great, infinite universe, descend for man's sake upon the earth, which certainly disappears into nothing before the immeasurable greatness and fullness of the universe ? What unworthy, mean, " human " imagination ! To concentrate

God upon earth, to plunge God into man, is about the same as to try to condense the ocean into one drop, to reduce the ring of Saturn into a finger-ring. Truly it is a rather narrow idea to think the universal being as limited only to earth or man, and to believe that Nature exists only on his account, that the sun shines only on account of the human eye. You do not see, however, short-sighted rationalist, that it is not the idea of God, but the idea of *Nature*, which within yourself objects to a union of God and man, and shows it to be a nonsensical contradiction; you do not see that the centre of union, *tertium comparationis*, between God and man is not that being to which you directly or indirectly attribute the power and effects of Nature, but rather *that* being which sees and hears, because you see and hear, which possesses consciousness, intellect and will, because you possess these faculties, or, in other words, that being which you distinguish from Nature, because you distinguish yourself from her. What, then, can you really object if this being finally appears as a real man before your eyes? How can you reject the consequences if you adhere to the premises ? How can you deny the son if you acknowledge the father ? If the God-man to you is a creature of human imagination and self-deification, then you must acknowledge, also, the creator of Nature to be a creature of human imagination and self-exaltation over Nature. If you wish for a being without any anthropomorphism, without any human additions, be they additions of the intellect, or the heart, or of imagination, then be courageous and consistent enough to give up God altogether, and to appeal only to pure, naked, godless nature as to the last basis of your existence. As long as you admit a *difference*, so long you incarnate in God your own difference, so long you *incorporate your own essence and nature in the universal and primary being ;* for *as you do not have nor know in distinction from human nature any other being than Nature, so, on the other hand, you neither have nor know any other being in distinction from Nature than the human one.*

§ 45. The conception of man's essence as an objective being different from man, or, in short, the personification of the human essence, has for its presupposition the incarnation of the objective being which is different from man, *i. e.* the conception of Nature as of a human being. ([16])   Will and intellect therefore appear to man as the primary powers or causes of Nature only because the unintentional effects of Nature appear to him in the light of his intellect as intentional ones, as ends and purposes; Nature herself consequently as an intelligent being (or at least as a mere thing of intellect).   As everything is seen by the sun—the God of the sun, " Hëlios " hears and sees everything—because man sees everything in the sunlight, so everything in itself has been thought, because man thinks it ; a work of intellect, because for him an object of his intellect.   Because he measures the stars and their distances, they are measured ; because he applies mathematics in order to understand Nature and her laws, they have also been applied to her production ; because he sees the end of a certain motion, the result of a certain development, the function of a certain organ, this end, function or result is in itself a foreseen one ; because he can imagine the opposite of the position or direction of a heavenly body, nay even numberless other directions, while at the same time he perceives that if this direction were changed, also a series of fruitful, benevolent consequences would be made impossible, so that he considers this series of consequences as the motive of that very direction: therefore such direction has really and originally been selected with admirable wisdom, and only with regard to its benevolent consequences, from the multitude of other directions which also exist only in man's head. Thus the principle of thinking is to man directly and without discrimination the principle of existence; the thing thought, the thing existing; the idea of the object, its essence, (the *a posteriori* the *a priori*.) Man thinks Nature otherwise than she really is; no wonder that he also presupposes as her cause and the cause of her existence another being than herself, a being which exists only in his mind, nay, which is even only the essence of his own mind. Man reverses the natural order of things; he founds the world in the very sense of the word upon its head, he makes the apex of the pyramid its basis—the first thing in or for the head, the reason why something is, the first thing in reality, the cause through which it exists. The motive of a thing precedes in the mind the thing itself. This is the reason why to man the essence of reason or intellect, the essence of thinking not only logically, but also physically, is the first, the primary being.

§ 46. The mystery of teleology is based upon the *contradiction* between the *necessity of Nature* and the *arbitrary will of man*, between Nature *such as she really is* and such *as man imagines her*. If the earth were placed somewhere else, if *e. g.* it were placed where Mercury now is, everything would perish in consequence of insupportable heat. How wisely, therefore, is the earth placed just where it appears best according to its quality. But in what does this wisdom consist? Only in the contradiction, in the contrast to *human folly*, which arbitrarily in thought places the earth somewhere else than where it is in reality. If you first *tear asunder* what in Nature is *inseparable*, as for instance the astronomical place of a heavenly body from its physical quality, then certainly the *unity* in Nature must *afterwards* appear to you as *expediency*, *necessity* as *plan*, the real and necessary place of a planet which agrees with its nature in contrast to the unfit one which you have thought of and chosen, as the *reasonable* one which has been justly *chosen* and wisely selected. " If the snow had a black color, or if such color prevailed in the arctic regions, all the arctic countries of the earth would be a gloomy desert, unfit for organic life. Thus the arrangement of the colors of bodies offers one of the most beautiful proofs for the wise arrangement of the world." Certainly, if man did not *change white into black*, if *human folly* had not disposed arbitrarily of Nature, no *divine wisdom* would rule over Nature.

§ 47. "Who has told the bird that it has only to raise its tail if it wants to fly downward, or to depress it, if it wants to ascend? He must be perfectly blind, who, in observing the flight of birds, does not perceive any higher wisdom *that has thought in their stead*." Certainly he must be blind, not for Nature, but for man, who makes *his nature* the *original* of Nature, the *power of intellect* the *original power*, who makes the birds' flight dependent upon *the insight* into the mechanical laws of flying, and who elevates his ideas abstracted from Nature into *laws* which the birds *apply* to their flight, just as the rider applies the rules of the art of riding, or the swimmer the rules of the art of swimming; with the only difference that to the birds the application of the art of flying is created with them. But the flight of birds is founded on no art. Art is only where also the *opposite* of art is to be found, where an organ performs a function which is not directly and necessarily connected with it, which does not exhaust its essence, and is only a *particular function by the side of many other real or possible* functions of the same organ. But the bird cannot fly otherwise than it does, nor is it at liberty not to fly; it *must* fly. The animal always knows how to do only that which it is able to do, and for this very reason it can do this one thing so perfectly, so masterly, so unsurpassably, because it does not know anything else, because its power is exhausted in this *one* function, because this one function is *identical with its nature.* If we therefore are unable to explain the actions and functions of the animals, especially those of the lower ones, which are endowed with certain artistic impulses, without presupposition of an intellect which has thought in their stead, this is only because we think that the objects of their activity are *objects* to them *in the same manner* as they are objects to our consciousness and intellect. As soon as we consider the works of the animals as *work of art*, as *arbitrary works*, we must necessarily also consider the intellect as their cause, for a work of art presupposes choice, intention, intellect, and consequently, as we know by experience that animals do not think themselves, *another* being as thinking *in their behalf.* [17] " Do you know how to advise the spider how it is to carry and to fasten the threads from one tree to another, from one housetop to another, from a height this side of the water to another one on the other side ?" Certainly not ; but do you indeed believe that there is any advice needed in this instance, that the spider is in the same condition

in which you would be, if you were to solve this problem
theoretically, that for it, as well as for you, there is any
difference between "this side" and "that side?" Between
the spider and the object to which it fastens the threads
of its net, there is as necessary a connection as between
your bone and muscle; for the object without it is for
it nothing but the support of its thread of life, as the
support of its fangs. The spider does not see what you
see; all the separations, differences and distances which,
or at least *such* as your intellectual eye perceives them,
do not at all exist for it. What therefore to you is an
insolvable *theoretical problem*, that is done by the spider
without any intellect, and consequently *without all
those difficulties* which exist only for your intellect.
"Who has told the vine-fretters that they find their
food in the fall of the year in greater abundance at the
branch and at the bud than at the leaf? Who has shown
them the way to the bud and to the branch? For the
vine-fretter which was born upon the leaf, the bud is not
only a distant but an entirely unknown province. I
adore the creator of the vine-fretter and of the cochineal
and remain silent." Certainly you must be silent if you
make the vine-fretters and cochineals preachers of
Theism, if *you endow them with your thoughts*, for only
to the vine-fretter *viewed from the standpoint of man*
is the bud a *distant and unknown* province, but not
to the vine-fretter itself, to which the leaf and the bud
are objects *not as such*, but only as matter which can be
assimilated and is chemically related to it. It is therefore only the *reflex of your eye* which shows you Nature
as *the work of an eye*, which obliges you to derive the
threads the spider draws from its *hind part*, from the
head of a thinking being. Nature is for you only a

spectacle, a delight of the eye; therefore you think that what delights your eye, also rules and moves Nature. Thus you make the *heavenly light* in which she appears to you, the *heavenly being* which has created her; the rays of the eye the lever of Nature; the *optic* nerve the *motory* nerve of the universe. To derive Nature from a wise creator is to produce children with a look; to satisfy hunger with the perfume of food; to move rocks by the harmony of sounds. If the Greenlander derives the shark's origin from human urine because it smells to man like it, this zoological genesis has the same foundation as as the cosmological genesis of the Theist, when he derives Nature from intellect, because she makes upon man the impression of intellect, and intention. Certainly the manifestation of Nature for us is reason, but the cause of such manifestation is as little reason as the cause of light is light.

§ 48. Why does Nature produce monsters? Because the result of a formation to her is not the object of a pre-existing purpose. Why supernumerary limbs? Because she does not number. Why does she place at the left hand side what generally lies on the right hand side, and vice versa? Because she does not know what is right or left. Monsters are therefore popular arguments, which for this very reason have been insisted on already by the Atheists of old, and even by such Theists as emancipated Nature from the guardianship of theology, in order to prove that the productions of Nature are unforeseen, unintentional, involuntary ones; for all reasons which are adduced for the sake of explaining monsters, even those of the most modern naturalists, according to which they are only consequences of diseases of the foetus, would be done away with, if with the creative or productive power of Nature at the same time will, intellect, forethought and consciousness were connected. But although Nature does not see, she is not therefore *blind;* although she does not live (in the sense of human, that is subjective, sensible life) she is not dead; and although she does not produce according to purposes, still her productions are not *accidental* ones; for where man defines Nature as dead and blind, and her productions as accidental ones, he defines her only so in *contrast to himself*, and declares her to be deficient because she does *not* possess what he possesses. Nature works and produces everywhere only in and with *connection*—a connection which is *reason* for man, for wherever he perceives connection, he finds sense, material for the thinking, "sufficient reason," system—only from and with *necessity*. But also the necessity of Nature is no human, *i. e.* no logical, metaphysical or mathematical, in general no abstracted one; for natural beings are no creatures of thought, no logical or mathematical figures, but real, sensual, individual beings; it is a sensual necessity and therefore eccentric, exceptional, irregular, which, in consequence of these anomalies of human imagination, appears even as freedom, or at least as a product of free will. Nature generally can be understood only *through herself;* she is that being whose idea depends on *no other* being; she alone admits of a discrimination between what a thing is *in itself* and what it is *for our conception;* she alone cannot be measured with any *human measure*, although we compare and designate her manifestations with analogous human manifestations in order to make them intelligible for us, and although in general we apply, and are obliged to apply to her, human expressions and ideas, such as order, purpose, in accordance with the nature of our language, which is founded only upon the subjective appearance of things.

§. 49. The religious admiration of divine wisdom in Nature is only an incident of enthusiasm ; it refers only to the *means*, but is extinguished in reflecting on the purposes of Nature. How wonderful is the spider's web, how wonderful the funnel of the ant-lion in the sand ! But what is the purpose of these wise arrangements ? Nothing but nourishment—a purpose which man in regard to himself degrades to a mere means. " Others," said Socrates—but these others are animals and brutish men— " others live in order to eat, but I eat in order to live." How magnificent is the flower, how admirable its structure ! But what is the purpose of this structure, of this magnificence ? Only to magnify and protect the genitals which man in himself either hides from shame, or even mutilates from religious zeal. " *The creator of the vine-fretters and of the cochineals*" whom the naturalist, the man of theory adores and admires, who has only natural life for his purpose, is therefore not the God and creator *in the sense of religion*. No! only the creator of man, and that of man such as he distinguishes himself from Nature, and rises above Nature, the creator in whom man has the *consciousness of himself*, in whom he finds represented the qualities which constitute his nature in distinction from external Nature, and *that in such a manner as he imagines them in religion*, is the God and creator such as he is an object of religion.

" The water" says Luther, " which is used in baptism and poured over the child *is also water not of the creator* but of *God the Saviour*." Natural water I have in common with animals and plants, but not the water of baptism ; the former amalgamates me with the other natural beings, the latter distinguishes me from them. But the object of religion is not natural water, but the water of baptism; consequently not the creator or author of natural, but of baptismal water is an object of religion. The creator of natural water is necessarily himself a natural, and therefore no religious, *i. e.* supernatural being. Water is a visible being, whose qualities and effects therefore do not lead us to a *supernatural* cause; but the baptismal water is no object for the *corporeal* eye, it is a spiritual, invisible, supersensuous being, *i. e.* one that exists and works only for faith, in thought, in imagination—a being which therefore requires also for its cause a spiritual being that exists only in faith and imagination. Natural water cleanses me only of my physical, but baptismal water of my moral impurities and diseases; the former only quenches my thirst for this temporal, transient life, but the latter satisfies my desire for life eternal; the former has only limited, defined, finite effects, but the latter infinite, all-powerful effects which surpass the nature of water, and which therefore represent and show the nature of the divine being, which is bound by no limit of Nature, the unlimited essence of man's power to believe and to imagine, bound to no limit of experience and reason. But is not also the creator of baptismal water the creator of natural water? In what relation therefore does the former stand to the latter? In the very same as baptismal to natural water; the former cannot exist if the latter does not exist; this one is the condition, the means of that one. Thus the creator of Nature is only *the condition for the creator of man.* How can he who does not hold the natural water in his hand combine with it supernatural effects? How can he who does not rule over temporal life give life eternal? How

can he whom the elements of Nature do not obey,
restore my body turned to dust? But who is the master
and ruler of Nature unless it be he who had power and
strength to produce her from naught by his mere will?
He, therefore, who declares the union of the supernatural
essence of baptism with natural water a contradiction,
without sense, may also declare the union of the supernatural essence of the creator with Nature such a contradiction; for between the effects of baptismal and common water is just as much or as little connection as
between the supernatural creator and natural Nature.
The creator comes from the same source from which the
supernatural, wonderful water of baptism gushes forth.
In the baptismal water we see only the essence of the
creator, of God, in a *sensible illustration*. How therefore can you reject the miracle of baptism and other
miracles, if you admit the essence of the creator, *i. e.* the
essence of the miracle? Or in other words: how can you
reject the *small* miracle if you admit the *great* miracle
of creation? But it is in the world of theology just as in
the political world; the small thieves are hanged, the
great ones are suffered to escape.

§ 50. That providence which is manifested in the
order, conformity to purpose and lawfulness of Nature, is not the providence of religion. The latter is
based upon liberty, the former upon necessity; the latter
is unlimited and unconditional, the former limited, depending on a thousand different conditions; the latter is
a special and individual one, the former is extended only
over the whole, the species, while the individual is left
to chance. A theistic naturalist says: "Many (or rather
all those in whose conception God was more than the
mathematical, imagined origin of Nature) have imagined

the preservation of the world and especially of mankind as *direct* and *special*, as if God ruled the actions of all creatures, and led them according to his pleasure. But after the consideration of the natural laws, we are unable to admit such a special government and superintendence over the actions of men and other creatures. . . We learn this from the little care which Nature takes of *single* individuals. (¹⁸) Thousands of them are sacrificed without hesitation or repentance in the plenty of Nature. . . Even with regard to man we make the same experience. Not one half of the human race reach the second year of their age, but die almost without having known that they ever lived. We learn this very thing also from the misfortunes and mishaps of all men, the good as well as the bad, which cannot well be made to agree with the special preservation or co-operation of the creator."

But a government, a providence which is no special one, does not answer to the purpose, the essence, the idea of providence; for providence is to destroy accident, but just that is upheld by a merely *general* providence which therefore is no better than *no* providence at all. Thus, *e. g.* it is a "law of divine order in Nature," *i. e.* a consequence of natural causes, that according to the number of years also the death of man occurs in a definite ratio ; that for instance, in the first year *one* child dies out of from three to four children, in the fifth year one out of twenty-five, in the seventh one out of fifty, in the tenth one out of one hundred, but still it is accidental, not regulated by this law, depending on other accidental causes, that just *this one* child dies, while those three or four others survive. Thus marriage is an "institution of God," a law of natural providence, in order to multiply the human race, and consequently a duty for me. But whether I

am to marry just *this one*, whether she is not perhaps in
consequence of an accidental organic deficiency unfit or
unproductive, that I am not told. But just because
natural providence, which in reality is nothing but
Nature herself, does not come to my assistance when I
come to apply the law to the special, single case, but
leaves me to myself just in the critical moment of decis-
ion, in the pressure of necessity; I appeal from her to a
higher court, to the *supernatural providence of the
Gods* whose eye shines upon me just where Nature's
light is extinguished; whose rule begins just where that
of natural providence is at an end. The Gods know and
tell me, they decide what Nature leaves in the darkness
of ignorance and gives up to accident. The region of
what commonly, as well as philosophically, is called accidental, "positive," individual, not to be foreseen, not
to be speculated upon, is the region of the Gods, the
region of religious providence. And oracles and prayer
are the religious means by which man makes the accidental, obscure, uncertain, an object of certainty, or at
least of hope. ([19])

§ 51. The Gods, says Epicurus, exist in the intervals
of the universe. Very well; they exist only in the void
space, in the abyss which is between the world of imagination and the world of reality, between the law and its
application, between the action and its result, between
the present and the future. The Gods are imagined
beings, beings of imagination which therefore owe also
their existence, strictly speaking, not to the present but
only to the *future* and the past. Those Gods who owe
their existence to the past, are those *who no longer exist,
the dead ones*, those beings which live only in mind and
imagination, whose worship among some nations consti-

tutes the whole religion, and with most of tnem an important essential part of religion. But far more mightily than by the past, is the mind influenced by the future; the former leaves behind only the quiet perception of remembrance, while the latter stands before us with the terrors of hell or the happiness of heaven. The Gods which rise from the tombs are therefore themselves only shades of Gods; the true living Gods, the rulers over rain and sunshine, lightning and thunder, life and death, heaven and hell, owe their existence likewise only to the powers of *fear* and *hope*, which rule over life and death, and which illuminate the dark abyss of the future with beings of the imagination. The present is exceedingly prosaic, ready made, determined, never to be changed, final, exclusive; in the present, imagination coincides with reality; in it therefore there is no place for the Gods; the present is godless. But the future is the empire of poetry, of unlimited possibility and accident—the future may be according to my wishes or fears; it is not yet subject to the stern lot of unchangeableness; it still hovers between existence and non-existence, high over "common" reality and palpability; it still belongs to *another* "*invisible*" world which is not put in motion by the laws of gravitation, but only by the sensory nerves. This world is the world of the Gods. Mine is the present, but the future belongs to the Gods. I am now; this present moment, although it will immediately be past, cannot be taken any more from me by the Gods; things that have happened cannot be undone even by divine power, as the ancients have already said. But shall I exist the *next* moment? Does the next moment of my life depend on my *will*, or is it in any *necessary* connection with the present one? No; a numberless multitude of accidents; the ground under my feet, the ceiling over my head, a flash of lightning, a bullet, a stone, even a grape which glides into my windpipe instead of passing into the æsophagus, can at any moment tear forever the coming moment from the present one. But the good Gods prevent this violent breach; they fill with their external, invulnerable bodies, the pores of the human body which are accessible to all possible destructive influences; they attach the coming moment to the one that is past; they unite the future with the present; they are, and possess in uninterrupted continuity, what men—the *porous* Gods—are and possess, only in intervals and with interruptions.

§ 52.   *Goodness* is an *essential* quality with the Gods; but how can they be good if they are not *almighty* and free from the laws of natural providence, *i. e.* from the fetters of natural necessity, if they do not appear in the individual instances which decide between life and death, as *masters of nature*, but as *friends* and *benefactors of men*, and if they consequently do *not* work *any miracles?* The Gods, or rather Nature, has endowed man with physical and mental powers in order to be able to sustain himself.   But are these natural means of sustaining himself *always* sufficient? Do I not frequently come into situations where I am lost without hope if no supernatural hand stops the inexorable course of natural order? The natural order is good, but is it *always* good? This continuous rain or drought *e. g.* is entirely in order; but must not I or my family, or even a whole nation perish in consequence of it, unless the Gods give their aid and stop it? ([20])   Miracles therefore are *inseparable* from the *divine* government and providence; nay, they are the only proofs, manifestations and revelations of the Gods, as of powers and beings distinguished from Nature ; to *deny* the *miracles* is to *deny the Gods themselves.* By what are Gods distinguished from men ? Only by their being *without* limits, what the latter are *in a limited manner,* and especially by their being *always* what the latter are only *for a certain time,* for a moment. ([21]) Men live—living existence is divinity, essential quality and primary condition of the Deity—but alas ! not for ever ; they die—but the Gods are the immortal ones who always live ; men are also happy, but not without interruption as the Gods ; men are also *good* but *not always,* and just this constitutes according to Socrates the difference between Deity and humanity, that the former is *always good ;* according to Aristotle, men also enjoy the divine happiness of thinking, but their mental activity is interrupted by other functions and actions. Thus the Gods and men have the same qualities and rules of life, only that the former possess them without, the latter with limitations and exceptions. As the life to come is nothing but *the continuation of this life uninterrupted by death,* so the divine being is nothing but *the continuation of the human being uninterrupted by Nature* in general—the *uninterrupted, unlimited* nature of man. But how are miracles distinguished from the effects of Nature ? Just as the Gods are distinguished from men. The miracle makes an effect or a quality of Nature which in a given case is not good, a good or at least a harmless one ; it causes that I do not sink and drown in the water, if I have the misfortune of falling into it ; that fire does not burn me ; that a stone, falling upon my head, does not kill me—in short, it makes that essence which now is beneficent, then destructive now philanthropic, then misanthropic, an essence

always good. The Gods and miracles owe their existence only to the exceptions of the rule. The Deity is
the destruction of the deficiencies and weaknesses in man
which are the very causes of the exceptions; the miracle
is the destruction of the deficiencies and limits in Nature.
The natural beings are defined and consequently limited
beings. This limit of theirs is in some abnormal cases
the cause of their injuriousness to man; but in the sense
of religion it is not a necessary one, but an arbitrary one,
made by God and therefore to be destroyed if necessity,
i. e. the welfare of man requires it.—To deny the miracles under the pretext that they are not becoming to
God's dignity and wisdom in virtue of which he has fixed
and determined everything from the beginning in the
best manner, is to sacrifice man to Nature, *religion to
intellect*, is to preach Atheism in the name of God. A
God who fulfills only such prayers and wishes of men as
can be fulfilled also *without him*, the fulfillment of which
is *within the limits and conditions of natural causes*,
who therefore helps only as long as art and Nature help,
but who ceases helping as soon as the materia medica is
at an end—such a God is nothing but the personified necessity of Nature hidden behind the name of God.

§ 53.   The belief in *God* is either the belief in Nature
(the objective being) as a human (subjective) being, or
the belief in the human essence as the essence of Nature.
The former is the natural religion, polytheism, ([22]) this
one spiritual or human religion, monotheism.   The polytheist sacrifices himself to Nature, he gives to the human
eye and heart the power and government over Nature;
the polytheist makes the human being dependent on
Nature, the monotheist makes Nature dependent on the
human being; the former says: *if Nature does not*

exist, I do not exist ; but the latter says vice versa: *if I do not exist, the world, Nature does not exist.* The first principle of religion is : *I am nothing compared with Nature, everything compared with me is God ;* everything inspires me with the feeling of dependence ; everything can bring me, although only accidentally, fortune and misfortune, welfare and destruction, (but man originally does not distinguish between cause and accidental motive); therefore everything is a motive of religion. Religion on the stand-point of such non-critical feeling of dependence is fetishism so-called, the basis of polytheism. But the conclusion of religion is : *everything is nothing compared with me*—all the magnificence of the stars, the supreme Gods of polytheism disappear before the magnificence of the human soul; all the power of the world before the power of the human heart ; all the necessity of dead unconscious Nature, before the necessity of the human, conscious being ; *for everything is only a means for me.* But Nature would not exist for me, if she existed *by herself*, if she were not from God. If she were by herself and therefore had the cause of her existence in herself, she would for this very reason have also an *independent* essence, an original existence and essence *without any relation to myself*, and independent from me. The signification of Nature according to which she appears to be *nothing for herself*, but only a *means for man*, is therefore to be traced back only to creation ; but this signification is manifested above all in those instances where man—as *e. g.* in distress, in danger of death—comes *into collision* with Nature, which however is sacrificed to man's welfare— in the miracles. Therefore the *premiss of the miracle is creation ; the miracle is the conclusion, the consequence, the truth of creation.* Creation is in the same relation to the miracle, as the species to the single individual; the miracle is the *act of creation* in a *special, single* case. Or, creation is *theory ;* its *practice* and *application* is the miracle. God is the *cause,* man the *end* of the world *i.e. God* is the *first being* in *theory,* but *man* is the *first being* in *practice.* Nature is nothing for God—nothing but a plaything of his power—but only in order that in an exigency, or rather generally, she is and can do nothing against man. In the creator man drops the limits of his essence, of his " soul," in the miracle the limits of his existence, of his body ; there he makes his invisible, thinking and reflected essence, here his individual, practical, visible essence, the essence of the world; then he *legitimates* the miracle; here he only *performs* it. The miracle accomplishes the end of religion in a sensual, popular way—the dominion of man over Nature, the *divinity* of man becomes a *palpable truth.* God works miracles, but upon man's prayer and although not upon an especial prayer, still in man's *sense,* in agreement with his most secret innermost wishes. Sarah laughed when in her old age the Lord promised her a little son, but nevertheless even then descendants were still her highest thought and wish. The *secret* worker of miracles therefore is man, but in the progress of time— time discloses every secret—he will and must become the *manifest,* visible worker of miracles. At first man *receives* miracles, finally he *works* miracles himself; at first he is the *object* of God, finally *God himself*; at first God only in heart, in mind, in thought, finally, God in flesh. But thought is bashful, sensuality without shame ; thought is silent and reserved, sensuality speaks out openly and frankly ; its utterances therefore are exposed to be ridi-

culed if they are contradictory to reason, because here
the contradiction is a visible, undeniable one. This is
the reason why the modern rationalists are ashamed to
believe in the God in the flesh *i. e.* in the sensual, visible
miracle, while they are not ashamed to believe in the
not-sensual God, *i. e.* in the not sensual, hidden miracle.
Still the time will come when the prophecy of Lichten-
berg will be fulfilled, and the belief in God in general,
consequently also the belief in a rational God will be considered as superstition just as well as already the belief
in the miraculous Christian God in flesh is considered as
superstition, and when therefore instead of the church light
of simple belief and instead of the twilight of rational-
istic belief, the pure light of Nature and reason will en-
lighten and warm mankind.

§ 54. He who for his God has no other material than
that which natural science, philosophy, or natural observation generally furnishes to him, who therefore con-
strues the idea of God from natural materials and considers him to be *nothing but the cause or the principle*
of the laws of astronomy, natural philosophy, geology, mineralogy, physiology, zoology and anthropology,
ought to be honest enough also to abstain from using the
name of God, for a *natural principle* is always a *natural essence* and *not what constitutes the idea of a God.*
([23]) As little as a church which has been turned into a
museum of natural curiosities, still is and can be called
a house of God, so little is a God really a God, whose
nature and efforts are only manifested in astronomical,
geological, anthropological works; God is a *religious word,
a religious object and being*, not a *physical*, astronomical, or in general a *cosmical* one. " *Deus et cultus*"says
Luther in his table-discourses, " *sunt relativa*," *God*

*and worship correspond to one another, one cannot be
without the other,* for *God must ever be the God of a
man or of a nation* and is always in *praedicamento
relationis,* both being in mutual relation to each other.
God will have some who adore and worship him; for to
have a God and to adore him correspond to each other,
sunt relativa, as *man* and *wife* in marriage—neither
can be without the other." God therefore presupposes
men who adore and worship him; God is a being the
idea or conception of whom does not depend on Nature
but on man, and that on religious man; an object of
adoration is not without an adoring being, i. e. God is
an object whose existence coincides with the existence of
religion, whose essence coincides with the essence of
religion, and which therefore does not exist *apart from
religion, different and independent from it,* but in whom
objectively is contained no more than what religion contains *subjectively.* (24) Sound is the *objective essence,*
the *God* of the ear; light is the *objective essence,* the
God of the eye; sound exists only for the ear, light only
for the eye; in the ear we have what we have in sound:
trembling, waving bodies, extended membranes, gelatin-
ous substances; but in the eye we have organs of light.
To make God an object of natural philosophy, astronomy
or zoology, is therefore just the same thing as making
sound an object of the eye. As the tone exists only in
the ear and for it, so God exists only in religion and for
it, *only in faith* and for it. As sound or tone as the
object of hearing expresses only the nature of the ear, so
God as an object *which is only the object of religion*
and faith, expresses the nature of religion and faith. But
what makes an object a *religious* one? As we have
seen, only man's imagination and mind. Whether you

worship Jehovah or Apis, the thunder or the Christ, your shadow, like the negro on the coast of Guinea, or your soul like the Persian of old, the *flatus ventris* or your genius—in short, whether you worship a sensual or spiritual being, it is all the same; something is an object of religion only *in so far* as it is an object of imagination and feeling, an object of faith; for just because the object of religion, such as it is its object, does not exist in reality, but rather contradicts the latter, for this very reason it is only an object of faith. Thus *e. g.* the immortality of man, or man as an immortal being is an object of religion, but for this very reason only an object of faith, for reality shows just the contrary, the mortality of man. To believe, means to *imagine* that something *exists* which does *not* exist; *e. g.* to imagine that a certain picture is a living being, that this bread is flesh, wine blood, *i. e.*, something *which it is not.* Therefore it betrays the greatest ignorance of religion if you hope to find God with the telescope in the sky of astronomy, or with a magnifying glass in a botanical garden, or with a mineralogic hammer in the mines of geology, or with the anatomic knife and microscope in the entrails of animals and men—you find him only in man's faith, imagination and heart; for God himself is nothing but the essence of man's imagination and heart.

§ 55. "As your heart, so is your God." *As the wishes of men, so are their Gods.* The Greeks had *limited Gods*—that means: they had *limited wishes.* The Greeks did not wish to live forever, they only wished not to grow old and die, and they did not absolutely wish not to die, they only wished not to die now — unpleasant things always come too soon for man—only not in the bloom of their age, only not of a

violent, painful death ; ([25]) they did not wish to be saved
in heaven, only happy, only to live without trouble and
pain ; they did not sigh as the Christians do, because
they were subject to the necessity of Nature, to the wants
of sexual instinct, of sleep, of eating and drinking; they
still submitted in their wishes to the limits of human nature ; they were not yet creators from nothing, they did
not yet make wine from water, they only purified and
distilled the water of Nature and changed it in an organic way into the blood of the Gods; they drew the
contents of divine and blissful life not from mere imagination, but from the materials of the real world; they
built the heaven of the Gods upon the ground of this
earth. The Greeks did not make the divine, *i. e.* the
possible being, the original and end of the real one, but
they made the real being the measure of the possible
one. Even when they had refined and spiritualized
their Gods by means of philosophy, their wishes were
founded upon the ground of reality and human nature.
The Gods are realized wishes; but the highest wish, the
highest bliss of the philosopher, of the thinker as such,
is to think undisturbed. The Gods of the Greek philosopher—at least of the Greek philosopher par excellence,
of the philosophical Jove, of Aristotle—are therefore undisturbed thinkers ; their happiness, their divinity, con-
sists in the uninterrupted activity of thinking. But this
activity, this happiness is itself a happiness, *real* within
this world, *within* human nature—although here limited
by interruptions—a defined, special, and therefore, in
the conception of Christians, limited and poor happiness
which is contradictory to the essence of true happiness;
for Christians have no limited but an unlimited God, surpassing all natural necessity, superhuman, extramundane

transcendental, *i. e.* they have *unlimited, transcendental wishes which go beyond the world, beyond Nature, beyond the essence of man — i. e. absolutely fantastic wishes.* Christians wish to be *infinitely greater and happier than the Gods* of the Olympus ; their wish is a heaven in which *all limits and all necessity of Nature are destroyed and all wishes are accomplished;* ([26]) a heaven in which there exist *no wants, no sufferings, no wounds, no struggles, no passions, no disturbances, no change of day and night, light and shade, joy and pain,* as in the heaven of the Greeks. In short the object of their belief is no longer a limited, defined God, a God with the determined name of Jove, or Pluto, or Vulcan, but God *without appellation,* because the object of their wishes is not a *named, finite, earthly* happiness, a determined enjoyment, such as the enjoyment of love, or of beautiful music, or of moral liberty, or of thinking, but an enjoyment which embraces all enjoyments, yet which for this very reason is a transcendental one, surpassing all ideas and thoughts, the enjoyment of an *infinite, unlimited, unspeakable, indescribable happiness.* Happiness and divinity are the same thing. Happiness as an object of belief, of imagination, generally as a theoretical object, is the Deity, the deity as an object of the heart, of the will, ([27]) of the wish as a practical object generally, is happiness. Or rather, the deity is an idea the truth and reality of which is only happiness. As far as the desire of happiness goes, so far, and no further, goes the idea of the deity. He who no longer has any supernatural wishes, has no longer any supernatural beings either.

(1) The theme of this treatise, or at least its starting point, is Religion, *inasmuch as its object is Nature*, which I was obliged to disregard in my "Essence of Christianity," since the centre of Christianity is not God *in Nature*, but God *in man*.—[Author's note].

(2) Nature, according to my conception, is nothing but a *general word* for denoting those beings, things and objects which man distinguishes from himself and his productions, and which he embraces under the common name of "Nature," but by no means a *general being*, abstracted and separated from the real objects and then personified into a mystical existence.

(3) All those qualities which originally are derived only from the contemplation of Nature, become in later times abstract, metaphysical qualities, just as Nature herself becomes an abstraction or creation of human reason. On this later standpoint, where man forgets the origin of God in Nature, when God no longer is an object of the senses, but an imaginary being, we must say: God without human qualities, who is to be distinguished from the properly human God, is nothing but the essence of reason. So much as regards the relation between this work and my former ones "Luther" and "The Essence of Christianity."

(4) This may be true in a logical sense, but never as far as the real genesis is concerned.

(5) It is self-evident that I do not intend to finally dispose in these few words of the great problem of the origin of organic life; but they are sufficient for my argument, as I give here only the indirect proof that life cannot have any other source but Nature. As regards the direct proofs of natural science, we are still far from the end, but in comparison with former times—especially in consequence of the lately proved identity of organic and inorganic phenomena—at least far enough to be able to be convinced of the natural origin of life, although the manner of this origin is yet unknown to us, or even if it never should be revealed unto us.

(6) Under this head we may also mention the many rules of etiquette which the ancient religions lay upon man in his intercourse with Nature, in order not to pollute or to violate her. Thus, *e. g.* no worshiper of Ormuzd was permitted to tread barefoot on the ground, because earth was sacred; no Greek was allowed to ford a river with unwashed hands.

(7) The expression for *to wish* is in the ancient German language the same as that for *to "enchant."*

(8) The Gods are blissful beings. The blessing is the result, the fruit, the end of an action which is independent from, but desired by me. "To bless" says Luther, "means to *wish some thing good.*" "If we bless, we do nothing else but *to wish something good*, but *we cannot give what we wish*; but God's blessing sounds fulfillment and soon proves its effect." That means : men are desiring beings ; the Gods are those beings which fulfill the desire. Thus even in common life the word God, so frequently used is nothing but the expression of a wish. "May God grant you children !" That means : I wish you children, with the only difference that the latter expression contains the wish as a subjective, not religious one, while the former implies it as an objective religious one.

(9) Thus in uncultivated times and among uncivilized nations religion may be a means of civilization, but in times of civilization religion represents the cause of rudeness, of antiquity, and is hostile to education.

(10) Under this head we may also consider the adoration of pernicious animals.

(11) Hesiod expressly says ; *also pheme* (*i. e.*, fame, rumor, public opinion) *is* a *deity*.

(12) The original kings, however, are well to be distinguished from the legitimate ones, so–called. The latter, except in some extraordinary instances, are ordinary individuals, insignificant in themselves, while the former were extraordinary, distinguished, *historical* individuals. The deification of distinguished men, especially after their death, forms therefore the most natural transition from the properly naturalistic religions to the mythological and anthropological ones, although it may also take place at the same time with natural adoration. The worshiping of distinguished men, however, is by no means confined to fabulous times. Thus the Swedes deified their king Erich at the time of Christianity and sacrificed unto him after his death.

(13) I range here the Greeks with the Israelites, while in my " Essence of Christianity " I contrast them with each other. This is by no means a logical contradiction, for things which, when compared with one another are different, coincide in comparison with a third thing. Besides, enjoyment of Nature includes also her *aesthetic, theoretical enjoyment.*

(14) An ecclesiastical writer expressively calls man " the tie of all things " (*syndesmon hapanton*), because God in him wished to embrace the universe into a unity, and because, therefore, in him all things as in their end are combined, and result in his advantage. And certainly man, as Nature's individualized essence, is her conclusion, but not in the anti-natural and supernatural sense of teleology and theology.

(15) This union, or the amalgamation of the "*moral*" and "*physical*" of the human and not human being, produces a *third*, which is neither Nature nor man, but which participates of both, like an amphibial, and which, for this very mystery of its nature, is the idol of mysticism and speculation.

(16) Viewed from this standpoint the creator of Nature is therefore nothing but the essence of Nature, which, by means of abstracting from Nature, has been distinguished and abstracted from Nature, and such as she is an object of the senses and by the power of imagination has been changed into a human or man-like being, and thus popularized, anthropomorphized, personified.

(17) Thus, generally, in all syllogisms from Nature to a God, the antecedent, the *presupposition* is a *human* one; no wonder therefore that their *result* is a *human being* or being *similar to man*. If the world is a machine there must necessarily be an architect. If the natural beings are as indifferent toward one another as the human individuals which can be employed and united only by means of higher power for any arbitrary purpose of state, as for instance war, there must naturally also be a ruler, a governor, a chief general of nature—a captain of the clouds —if she shall not be dissolved into nothing. Thus man first makes Nature unconsciously a *human work, i. e.* he makes his essence her fundamental essence, but as he afterwards or at the same time perceives the difference between the works of Nature and those of human art, his own essence appears to him as another, but analogous, similar one. All arguments for God's existence have therefore only a logical or rather anthropological signification, since also the logical forms are forms of human nature.

(18) Nature however "cares " just as little for the species or genus. The latter is preserved because it is nothing but the totality of the individuals which

by coition propagate and multiply themselves. While single individuals are exposed to accidental, destructive influences, others escape them. The plurality is thus preserved. But still, or rather from the same reasons which cause the single individual to perish, even species die away. Thus the Dronte has disappeared, thus the Irish gigantic deer, thus even now-a-days many animal species disappear in consequence of man's persecution and of the evermore extending civilization in from regions where they once or even a short time ago still existed in great numbers, as, e. g. the seal from some inlands ; and in time will disappear entirely from the earth.

(19) Compare in regard to this matter the expressions of Socrates in Xenophon's writings as to oracles.

(20) The Christians pray likewise to their God for rain as the Greeks did to Jove, and believe that they are heard with such prayers. "There was," says Luther, in his table-discourses, "a great drought, as it had not rained for a long time, and the grain in the field began to dry up when Dr. M. L. prayed continually and said finally with heavy sighs: O, Lord, pray regard our petition in behalf of thy promise.......I know that we cry to thee and sigh desirously; why dost thou not hear us ? And the very next night came a very fine fruitful rain."

(21) It is true the omission of the limits has increase and change for its consequences ; but it does not destroy the essential identity.

(22) The definition of polytheism generally and without further explanation as natural religion, holds good only relatively and comparatively.

(23) Arbitrariness in the use of words is unbounded. But still no words are used so arbitrarily, nor taken in so c ntradictory significations as the words *God* and *religion*. Whence this arbitrariness and confusion? Because people from reverence or from fear to contradict opinions sanctioned by age, retain the old names (for only *the name, the appearance, rules the world, even the world of believers in God*), although they connect *entirely different* ideas with them which have been gained only in the course of time. Thus it was in regard to the Grecian Gods which in the course of time received the most contradictory significations ; thus in regard to the Christian God, Atheism *calling* itself theism is the religion, anti-Christianity calling itself Christianity is the true Christianity of the present day.—*Mundus vult decipi.*

(24) A being therefore which is only a philosophical principle, and consequently only an object of philosophy, but not of religion, of worship. of prayer, of the heart ; a being that does not accomplish any wishes, nor hear a y prayers, is only a nominal God, but not a God in reality.

(25) While therefore in the paradise of Christian phantasms man could not die and would not die if he had not sinned, with the Greeks man died even in the blissful age of Kronos, but as easily as if he fell asleep. In this idea the natural wish of man is realized. Man does not wish for immortal life; he only wishes for a long life of physical and mental health and a painless death agreeable to Nature. To resign the belief in immortality requires nothing less than an inhuman Stoic resignation; it requires nothing but to be convinced that the articles of the Christian creed are founded only upon supernaturalistic, fantastic wishes, and to return to the simple real nature of man,

(26) Luther e.g. says : "But where God is (i.e. in heaven) there must also be all good things which even we may possibly wish for." Thus in the Koran, according to Savary's translation it is said of the inhabitants of Paradise : " *Tous leurs desirs seront combles.*" (All their wishes will be accomplished.) Only their wishes are of a different kind.

(27) The will however, especially in the sense of the moralists, does not constitute the specific essence of religion ; because what I can attain by my will, for that I need no Gods. To make morals the essential cause of religion is to retain the name of religion, but to drop its essence. One can be moral without God, but happy—in the supernaturalistic, Christian sense of the word—one cannot be without God ; for happiness in this sense lies beyond the limits and the power of Nature and mankind, it therefore presupposes for its realization a supernatural being which is and can do, what is impossible to Nature and mankind. If Kant therefore made morals the essence of religion, he was in the same or at least a similar relation to Christian religion as Aristotle to the Greek religion, when the latter made theory the essence of the Gods. As little as a God who is only a speculative being, nothing but intellect, still is a *God*, so little a merely moral being or a "personified law of morals" is still a God. It is true, Jove already is also a philosopher, when he looks smilingly down from Olympus upon the struggles of the Gods, but he is still infinitely more ; certainly also the Christian God is a moral being, but still infinitely more ; morals are only the condition of happiness. The true idea which is at the bottom of Christian happiness, especially in contrast to philosophic heathenism, is however no other than the one, that true happiness can be found only in the gratification of man's *whole* nature, for which reason Christianity admits also the body, the flesh, to the participation in the divinity or what is the same thing, in the enjoyment of happiness. But the development of this thought does not belong here, it belongs to the "Essence of Christianity."

GREAT BOOKS IN PHILOSOPHY PAPERBACK SERIES

ESTHETICS

☐ Aristotle—*The Poetics*
☐ Aristotle—*Treatise on Rhetoric*

ETHICS

☐ Aristotle—*The Nicomachean Ethics*
☐ Marcus Aurelius—*Meditations*
☐ Jeremy Bentham—*The Principles of Morals and Legislation*
☐ John Dewey—*Human Nature and Conduct*
☐ John Dewey—*The Moral Writings of John Dewey, Revised Edition*
☐ Epictetus—*Enchiridion*
☐ David Hume—*An Enquiry Concerning the Principles of Morals*
☐ Immanuel Kant—*Fundamental Principles of the Metaphysic of Morals*
☐ John Stuart Mill—*Utilitarianism*
☐ George Edward Moore—*Principia Ethica*
☐ Friedrich Nietzsche—*Beyond Good and Evil*
☐ Plato—*Protagoras, Philebus, and Gorgias*
☐ Bertrand Russell—*Bertrand Russell On Ethics, Sex, and Marriage*
☐ Arthur Schopenhauer—*The Wisdom of Life* and *Counsels and Maxims*
☐ Adam Smith—*The Theory of Moral Sentiments*
☐ Benedict de Spinoza—*Ethics* and *The Improvement of the Understanding*

LOGIC

☐ George Boole—*The Laws of Thought*

METAPHYSICS/EPISTEMOLOGY

☐ Aristotle—*De Anima*
☐ Aristotle—*The Metaphysics*
☐ Francis Bacon—*Essays*
☐ George Berkeley—*Three Dialogues Between Hylas and Philonous*
☐ W. K. Clifford—*The Ethics of Belief and Other Essays*
☐ René Descartes—*Discourse on Method* and *The Meditations*
☐ John Dewey—*How We Think*
☐ John Dewey—*The Influence of Darwin on Philosophy and Other Essays*
☐ Epicurus—*The Essential Epicurus: Letters, Principal Doctrines, Vatican Sayings, and Fragments*
☐ Sidney Hook—*The Quest for Being*
☐ David Hume—*An Enquiry Concerning Human Understanding*
☐ David Hume—*Treatise of Human Nature*
☐ William James—*The Meaning of Truth*
☐ William James—*Pragmatism*
☐ Immanuel Kant—*The Critique of Judgment*
☐ Immanuel Kant—*Critique of Practical Reason*
☐ Immanuel Kant—*Critique of Pure Reason*
☐ Gottfried Wilhelm Leibniz—*Discourse on Metaphysics* and the *Monadology*
☐ John Locke—*An Essay Concerning Human Understanding*
☐ George Herbert Mead—*The Philosophy of the Present*

- ❏ Charles S. Peirce—*The Essential Writings*
- ❏ Plato—*The Euthyphro, Apology, Crito,* and *Phaedo*
- ❏ Plato—*Lysis, Phaedrus,* and *Symposium*
- ❏ Bertrand Russell—*The Problems of Philosophy*
- ❏ George Santayana—*The Life of Reason*
- ❏ Sextus Empiricus—*Outlines of Pyrrhonism*
- ❏ Ludwig Wittgenstein—*Wittgenstein's Lectures: Cambridge, 1932–1935*
- ❏ Alfred North Whitehead—*The Concept of Nature*

PHILOSOPHY OF RELIGION

- ❏ Jeremy Bentham—*The Influence of Natural Religion on the Temporal Happiness of Mankind*
- ❏ Marcus Tullius Cicero—*The Nature of the Gods* and *On Divination*
- ❏ Ludwig Feuerbach—*The Essence of Christianity* and *The Essence of Religion*
- ❏ Paul Henry Thiry, Baron d'Holbach—*Good Sense*
- ❏ David Hume—*Dialogues Concerning Natural Religion*
- ❏ William James—*The Varieties of Religious Experience*
- ❏ John Locke—*A Letter Concerning Toleration*
- ❏ Lucretius—*On the Nature of Things*
- ❏ John Stuart Mill—*Three Essays on Religion*
- ❏ Friedrich Nietzsche—*The Antichrist*
- ❏ Thomas Paine—*The Age of Reason*
- ❏ Bertrand Russell—*Bertrand Russell On God and Religion*

SOCIAL AND POLITICAL PHILOSOPHY

- ❏ Aristotle—*The Politics*
- ❏ Mikhail Bakunin—*The Basic Bakunin: Writings, 1869–1871*
- ❏ Edmund Burke—*Reflections on the Revolution in France*
- ❏ John Dewey—*Freedom and Culture*
- ❏ John Dewey—*Individualism Old and New*
- ❏ John Dewey—*Liberalism and Social Action*
- ❏ G. W. F. Hegel—*The Philosophy of History*
- ❏ G. W. F. Hegel—*Philosophy of Right*
- ❏ Thomas Hobbes—*The Leviathan*
- ❏ Sidney Hook—*Paradoxes of Freedom*
- ❏ Sidney Hook—*Reason, Social Myths, and Democracy*
- ❏ John Locke—*Second Treatise on Civil Government*
- ❏ Niccolo Machiavelli—*The Prince*
- ❏ Karl Marx (with Friedrich Engels)—*The German Ideology,* including *Theses on Feuerbach* and *Introduction to the Critique of Political Economy*
- ❏ Karl Marx—*The Poverty of Philosophy*
- ❏ Karl Marx/Friedrich Engels—*The Economic and Philosophic Manuscripts of 1844* and *The Communist Manifesto*
- ❏ John Stuart Mill—*Considerations on Representative Government*
- ❏ John Stuart Mill—*On Liberty*
- ❏ John Stuart Mill—*On Socialism*

- ☐ John Stuart Mill—*The Subjection of Women*
- ☐ Montesquieu, Charles de Secondat—*The Spirit of Laws*
- ☐ Friedrich Nietzsche—*Thus Spake Zarathustra*
- ☐ Thomas Paine—*Common Sense*
- ☐ Thomas Paine—*Rights of Man*
- ☐ Plato—*Laws*
- ☐ Plato—*The Republic*
- ☐ Jean-Jacques Rousseau—*Émile*
- ☐ Jean-Jacques Rousseau—*The Social Contract*
- ☐ Mary Wollstonecraft—*A Vindication of the Rights of Men*
- ☐ Mary Wollstonecraft—*A Vindication of the Rights of Women*

GREAT MINDS PAPERBACK SERIES

ART

- ☐ Leonardo da Vinci—*A Treatise on Painting*

CRITICAL ESSAYS

- ☐ Desiderius Erasmus—*The Praise of Folly*
- ☐ Jonathan Swift—*A Modest Proposal and Other Satires*
- ☐ H. G. Wells—*The Conquest of Time*

ECONOMICS

- ☐ Charlotte Perkins Gilman—*Women and Economics: A Study of the Economic Relation between Women and Men*
- ☐ John Maynard Keynes—*The General Theory of Employment, Interest, and Money*
- ☐ John Maynard Keynes—*A Tract on Monetary Reform*
- ☐ Thomas R. Malthus—*An Essay on the Principle of Population*
- ☐ Alfred Marshall—*Money, Credit, and Commerce*
- ☐ Alfred Marshall—*Principles of Economics*
- ☐ Karl Marx—*Theories of Surplus Value*
- ☐ John Stuart Mill—*Principles of Political Economy*
- ☐ David Ricardo—*Principles of Political Economy and Taxation*
- ☐ Adam Smith—*Wealth of Nations*
- ☐ Thorstein Veblen—*Theory of the Leisure Class*

HISTORY

- ☐ Edward Gibbon—*On Christianity*
- ☐ Alexander Hamilton, John Jay, and James Madison—*The Federalist*
- ☐ Herodotus—*The History*
- ☐ Thucydides—*History of the Peloponnesian War*
- ☐ Andrew D. White—*A History of the Warfare of Science with Theology in Christendom*

LAW

- ☐ John Austin—*The Province of Jurisprudence Determined*

PSYCHOLOGY

☐ Sigmund Freud—*Totem and Taboo*

RELIGION

☐ Thomas Henry Huxley—*Agnosticism and Christianity and Other Essays*
☐ Ernest Renan—*The Life of Jesus*
☐ Upton Sinclair—*The Profits of Religion*
☐ Elizabeth Cady Stanton—*The Woman's Bible*
☐ Voltaire—*A Treatise on Toleration and Other Essays*

SCIENCE

☐ Jacob Bronowski—*The Identity of Man*
☐ Nicolaus Copernicus—*On the Revolutions of Heavenly Spheres*
☐ Francis Crick—*Of Molecules and Men*
☐ Marie Curie—*Radioactive Substances*
☐ Charles Darwin—*The Autobiography of Charles Darwin*
☐ Charles Darwin—*The Descent of Man*
☐ Charles Darwin—*The Origin of Species*
☐ Charles Darwin—*The Voyage of the Beagle*
☐ René Descartes—*Treatise of Man*
☐ Albert Einstein—*Relativity*
☐ Michael Faraday—*The Forces of Matter*
☐ Galileo Galilei—*Dialogues Concerning Two New Sciences*
☐ Ernst Haeckel—*The Riddle of the Universe*
☐ William Harvey—*On the Motion of the Heart and Blood in Animals*
☐ Werner Heisenberg—*Physics and Philosophy:*
    The Revolution in Modern Science
☐ Julian Huxley—*Evolutionary Humanism*
☐ Thomas H. Huxley—*Evolution and Ethics and Science and Morals*
☐ Edward Jenner—*Vaccination against Smallpox*
☐ Johannes Kepler—*Epitome of Copernican Astronomy*
    and Harmonies of the World
☐ Charles Mackay—*Extraordinary Popular Delusions*
    and the Madness of Crowds
☐ James Clerk Maxwell—*Matter and Motion*
☐ Isaac Newton—*Opticks, Or Treatise of the Reflections,*
    Inflections, and Colours of Light
☐ Isaac Newton—*The Principia*
☐ Louis Pasteur and Joseph Lister—*Germ Theory and Its Application*
    to Medicine and *On the Antiseptic Principle of the Practice of Surgery*
☐ William Thomson (Lord Kelvin) and Peter Guthrie Tait—
    The Elements of Natural Philosophy
☐ Alfred Russel Wallace—*Island Life*

SOCIOLOGY

☐ Emile Durkheim—*Ethics and the Sociology of Morals*